Origami Kit
FOR
DUMMIES®

by Nick Robinson

WILEY

A John Wiley and Sons, Ltd, Publication

Origami Kit For Dummies®
Published by
John Wiley & Sons, Ltd
The Atrium
Southern Gate
Chichester
West Sussex
PO19 8SQ
England

E-mail (for orders and customer service enquires): cs-books@wiley.co.uk

Visit our Home Page on www.wiley.com

Copyright © 2008 John Wiley & Sons, Ltd, Chichester, West Sussex, England

Published by John Wiley & Sons, Ltd, Chichester, West Sussex

For general information on our other products and services, please contact our Customer Care Department within the U.S. at 800-762-2974, outside the U.S. at 317-572-3993, or fax 317-572-4002.

For technical support, please visit www.wiley.com/techsupport.

Wiley also publishes its books in a variety of electronic formats. Some content that appears in print may not be available in electronic books.

The origami models in this book are reproduced by kind permission of: Anita Barbour (Dragonfly), Boaz Shuval (Butterfly), Dave Brill (Pentagonal Star), David Lister (Four Thirsty Birds), David Petty (60 Degree Star), Doris Lauinger (Giftbag), Edwin Corrie (Biscuit Packet Closure, Emblem), Eric Joisel (Dragon), Eric Kenneway (Hearts, reproduced by permission of the British Origami Society), Gay Merrill Gross (Vase), Grzegorz Bubniak (Beetle), Guspath Go (Mouse), Jeff Beynon (Twist Decoration), John Montroll (Chair), Kunihiko Kasahara (Chick), Luis Fernandez Perez (Perro Liberando), Makoto Yamaguchi (Makotokoma), Mark Kirschenbaum (Pureland Person), Martin Wall (Boat), Max Hulme (Aladdin), Michael LaFosse (Sailboat Envelope), Michel Grand (A Fishy Tale, Face Envelope), Mike Dilkes (Miniphant), Nick Robinson (Ali's Dish, Bookmark, Container, Droodle, Duck, Dummyman, Dunce's Cap, Elephant's Head, Fish sequence, Flood Bowl, Fox Head, Gomez Bowl, Hexahedron, Japanese Schoolgirl, Jaws Fin, Lazy Winston, Little Nicky, Modular Star, Mystery Fold, Shining Heart, Triplane), Paul Jackson (3 Crease Head), Peter Borcherds (Tulip Bowl), Sylvia Shen (4 Compartment Box), Rachel Katz (3D Star), Robert Lang (Snail), Robert Neale (Lovebirds), Robin Glynn (Dracula), Rocky Jardes (Fluted Module), Roman Diaz (Chinese

Frog), Stephen Casey (Goldfish, Shell), Ted Norminton (Santa), Thoki Yenn (Butterfly, reproduced by permission of Thomas Søndergaard on behalf of Thoki Yenn), Tony O'Hare (Hen), Wayne Brown (Envelope, House, Foxes Head), Yoshihide Momotani (Twist Flower).

British Library Cataloguing in Publication Data: A catalogue record for this book is available from the British Library

ISBN: 978-0-470-75857-1

Printed and bound in Great Britain by Clays Ltd

10 9 8 7 6 5 4 3

WILEY

About the Author

Nick Robinson has been folding paper since the early 1980s and has been a member of the British Origami Society (BOS) for over 25 years. He served on the BOS council for over 20 years, edited their bimonthly magazine for 5 years, and still maintains their website. In 2004 he was awarded the Sidney French medal — the highest award the society can offer — in recognition of his outstanding contribution to origami. Nick spent many years as a professional origami teacher, travelling around schools, libraries, youth clubs, hospitals, and art galleries, teaching origami and paper artwork. He ran sessions with people of all ages and physical abilities.

Nick has appeared on television and has fulfilled numerous commissions for magazines, television, and Internet advertising campaigns. Over 200 of his original origami creations have been published in 13 countries around the world, including a Japanese newspaper. He has submitted work to many prestigious exhibitions around the world. In 1994, Nick won three of the five categories for the International Alice in Wonderland Origami competition. He has been invited as a special guest to origami conventions in Switzerland, Germany, Italy, France, Austria, America, and Japan. Nick has written and illustrated 25 origami books, with total worldwide sales of several million. His origami website is www.origami.me.uk.

Nick is in his very early 50s with a BA honours degree in communication studies. He lives in Sheffield, England, with his wife Alison, grown-up children Daisy and Nick, plus cats Gomez and Matilda. As a former professional musician he still performs solo improvised ambient guitar concerts. His music website is www.looping.me.uk. When not folding paper or making music, Nick likes to watch tadpoles in his garden pond, cycle in the countryside, eat curries, make awful puns, take photographs, and generally embarrass his children.

Author's Acknowledgements

This book is dedicated to my beautiful Alison, Daisy, and Nick Jnr (arguably taller than his dad now). Also to our cats Matilda and Gomez, who is 21 years old and looking every day of his age.

Special thanks to the origami designers whose models appear in this book, for their generosity in allowing me to publish their work and for offering advice and ideas.

More general thanks to Wayne Brown for friendship, proof-reading, and most importantly telling me when I'm being an arse. Origami-l and BOSmail mailing lists for ideas and feedback. Florence Temko, Robert Lang, Edwin Corrie, Eric Joisel, Dave Venables, and Dave Brill for feedback, support, and assistance. Joan Homewood, Penny

Groom, Mick Guy, and Ann Lavin for spiritual support during a recent illness. Bev, Steve, John, Rich, Chris, and Dave, my fellow band-members, for helping me to make beautiful(?) music. Roger Price for the wonderful world of droodles; The Dilshad and Shimul Indian restaurants for me spicy wittals. All at Cherry Red Records. Matt and Folding Australia for vital information about bricks. Dennis Walker for proofing, songs, and humour. Thea and Darren, the 'other' Sheffield folders. All at Charnock Health Centre, Sheffield. OUSA for the invite; sorry I couldn't make it! My other origami friends are entirely too numerous to mention, but you know who you are and I thank you!

If I've forgotten anyone (and I generally do), sincere apologies.

On the *For Dummies* side, thanks to Rachael, Wejdan, and Sarah at Wiley.

His work is unbelievable!

— Eric Joisel

I can think of nobody better qualified to write this book.

— Robert Lang

Publisher's Acknowledgements

We're proud of this book; please send us your comments through our Dummies online registration form located at www.dummies.com/register/.

Some of the people who helped bring this book to market include the following:

Acquisitions, Editorial, and Media Development

Development Editor: Rachael Chilvers

Content Editor: Nicole Burnett

Proofreader: Kim Vernon

Technical Editor: Holly Myers

Commissioning Editor: Wejdan Ismail

Publisher: Jason Dunne

Executive Project Editor: Daniel Mersey

Cover Photos: © Jeffrey Coolidge/ GettyImages

Cartoons: Rich Tennant (www.the5thwave.com)

Composition Services

Project Coordinators: Erin Smith, Lynsey Stanford

Layout and Graphics: Reuben Davis, Brooke Graczyk, Melissa K. Jester, Laura Pence

Proofreaders: Laura Albert, David Faust

Indexer: Ty Koontz

Publishing and Editorial for Consumer Dummies

    Diane Graves Steele, Vice President and Publisher, Consumer Dummies

    Kristin Ferguson-Wagstaffe, Product Development Director, Consumer Dummies

    Ensley Eikenburg, Associate Publisher, Travel

    Kelly Regan, Editorial Director, Travel

Publishing for Technology Dummies

    Andy Cummings, Vice President and Publisher, Dummies Technology/General User

Composition Services

    Gerry Fahey, Vice President of Production Services

    Debbie Stailey, Director of Composition Services

Contents at a Glance

Table of Contents

Introduction

● ●

I've been learning and loving origami for nearly 30 years. What got me started? Buried deep within me was a desire to learn a creative art. I tried basket-weaving, macramé, and painting, but found no real empathy with those subjects. When I borrowed my first origami book from the library, I quickly realised I'd found what I was looking for. A perfect marriage of art and technique, origami enables you to turn innocent sheets of paper into little gems that you can give to other people, brightening up both your lives.

The joy of origami, the art of paper-folding, lies partly in an innate human need to fiddle with paper. You get a bus ticket and can't leave it alone. You fold it in half, form a tube, make pleats – it seems impossible not to. Fiddling about with paper is also a way of magically transforming an everyday material into a living, breathing creation. People are always amazed at the possibilities of the humble sheet of paper when you use it for origami. You don't need to be a genius or artist to make or design origami models, nor do you need an endless supply of patience. As you'll see in this book, you can make a recognisable origami model in a few seconds.

To a convert, origami is more than just folding paper – it's an expression of fundamental human values: creativity, curiosity, emotion, communication, and above all, fun!

About This Book

The possible origami creations are endless, from flowers to birds, from cars to cuckoo clocks, from dung-beetles to elephants. For this book I've selected designs from a wide variety of subject areas and ordered them according to complexity. Where appropriate, I try to explain the thinking behind some of the steps, as well as the way in which origami diagrams and symbols are used to explain a three-dimensional move in what is a necessarily flat drawing. I also inject the odd note of humour; partly to avoid the accusation that origami books have to be dry, but mainly because that's the kind of guy I am and it's far too late to change.

Throughout this book, I encourage you to be creative and to experiment with the models; changing angles, distances, and so on to see what you can discover. Just because the model is called a goldfish doesn't mean you can't adapt it to become a herring or a whale.

You may feel that a particular model can be improved by a few shaping moves at the end, and this is as it should be – go ahead and make your moves! The world needs new creative folders! However, even if you feel you don't have a creative bone in your body, simply following the instructions will make everyone else think you're very talented, so don't debate the point, just show them the model and bask in the praise.

Conventions Used in This Book

To make this book even easier to use I use a few conventions. The action parts of the numbered steps are in **bold** and the numbers correspond to the numbers in the accompanying illustrations. (Well, it would be a bit confusing if they didn't.) Web and email addresses are in `monofont`.

Most origami models are created by real live human beings and I credit them whenever appropriate. Doing so is polite, legally advisable, and it's good to associate the model with the creator's name.

Origami instruction symbols can have subtle differences. I explain the symbols I use in Chapter 1, and use them consistently throughout the book. I also include them on the cheat sheet so you can refer to them quickly and easily.

You can fold everything in this book from a standard 15-centimetre-square piece of paper (but feel free to go larger or smaller as you like). However, for the more challenging designs in Chapters 6 and 7, you may want to double this size until you're confident with the model.

What to call someone who practises origami? The terms 'origamist', 'paper-folder', 'paper-artist', 'origamian', and *'plieur de papier'* are all in use, but I prefer the first, because it's not too posh, and has right air of implied competence about it.

Foolish Assumptions

In writing this book I couldn't help but make a few assumptions about you, dear reader. I assume that:

- ✔ You want to get to grips with the fundamentals (and more) of origami.
- ✔ You have no previous knowledge of origami and want me to take you step-by-step through all the techniques and terms you'll need to become a fully-qualified paper-folder.

    ✔ You may have already dipped your toe into papery water and want to discover more models to fully immerse yourself in.

Put simply, this book is for anyone remotely interested in the endless possibilities and enjoyment of origami.

How This Book Is Organised

This book is divided into three parts; the need-to-know stuff, the models, and the fun tips and information at the end.

Part I: Coming to the Crease: Basic Techniques

In this part I introduce you to the essential techniques and symbols you need to start folding.

I explain how to create your own models and make your own origami instructions, which can actually help you to become a better folder. In addition, you can share your efforts with the rest of the origami world and be a contributor rather than just a user. I describe a variety of techniques ranging from very low to hi-tech. I also explore origami ethics. Intrigued? It's all in Chapter 2!

Part II: Folding On: The Models

This part is where you'll find 75 models to create, ranging from designs that use the simplest of techniques through to those with many separate steps. From simple and moderate models you move on to geometric and challenging designs. Don't panic – you don't need to understand *any* mathematics in order to complete the geometric models. Maths isn't one of my strong points!

Also in this part, you'll meet some origami *bases*, straightforward folding sequences common to many designs. I use simple designs within the information about bases to demonstrate the techniques.

Part III: The Part of Tens

In this set of small but perfectly formed chapters you'll find a series of origami nuggets to enhance your enjoyment and skill. Discover my top ten folders, check out top tips to try, and experiment with ten different styles of origami.

Icons Used in This Book

Scattered throughout the book are icons to help you navigate to certain key bits of information.

The folded paper knot draws your attention to a key point about origami to bear in mind.

This icon highlights a spot where a little more concentration or subtlety is required to make a really job of a model. As well as using in within the written instructions, I also use it occasionally within the figures.

Ouch! Avoid these potential origami pitfalls.

The target arrow highlights a particularly useful piece of advice.

Where to Go from Here

You can dip in and out of the book as you like, but I recommend that you follow the traditional route from easier models to more difficult to build up your experience. Success with a simple design encourages you when you come to the more challenging models in the book. If you want to find a particular model or technique you can use the table of contents and the index in the back of this book.

Origami has never been a super trendy activity, and you may need to develop a forgiving attitude in case your friends scoff at your hobby, but once you've mastered a few simple designs, they'll sit back in amazement and you'll become everyone's best friend. Well, perhaps.

Part I

Coming to the Crease: Basic Techniques

This doesn't look good for O'Brien. As you know, Takahashi is an expert in Judo, Tai Kwan Do, and origami.

In this part . . .

Welcome to Part I, where I initiate you into the marvellous and mysterious techniques and symbols you need to start folding and making models.

In this part you'll also discover how to create your own models and write your own origami instructions.

Chapter 1

Getting Started in Origami

In This Chapter

▶ Finding folding materials

▶ Discovering origami symbols

*M*aking an origami design, whether simple or complex, generally requires concentration and accurate folding. In order to
achieve these desirable aims, you need to create the proper environment in which to fold, as well as observing a few basic guide-
lines about how to fold. This chapter explores the things to think
about before you get stuck in to the origami models – the materials
and tools you need (sometimes more than paper and hands are
useful!). This chapter also introduces you to the symbols that
show you what folds and creases to make, not to mention how to
tell when you need to rotate the paper and apply pressure.

The following tips assume you're improving your folding skills by
working on new material – clearly, after you've learned a design
you can (and will) fold it anywhere!

Origami through the ages

As with many ancient arts, historians don't know for certain when origami began.
Paper was invented during the second century AD in China, so it's likely that's where
the art of folding paper first started. Japan began to produce paper a little later and
origami as we know it was developed in Japan. Used initially for ceremonial events,
recreational origami grew slowly until about 150 years ago when things really
took off.

The principles of creative origami were developed by Japanese masters such as
Akira Yoshizawa and Kosho Uchiyama and during the 1950s, and by Westerners
Robert Harbin, Gershon Legman, and Sam Randlett. They set in place the method of
diagramming used today and made huge efforts to forge links between previously
isolated folders in order to develop a proper community of origamists.

Folding Here, There, and (Nearly) Everywhere

So where and when should you fold? When to make an origami model depends on your individual circumstances, but it's generally not a good idea to tackle a new project at 3 o'clock in the morning after a 12-hour shift. Try to find a gap in your schedule where you can devote at least half an hour to folding without having to take breaks to wash the dishes or stroke the cat.

Consider where you're going to fold. Ideally you want a large flat table with plenty of elbow-room, somewhere to spread out the instructions or book, and good lighting. Don't forget to have a waste-paper basket handy in case your first efforts get a bit mangled, and keep on hand some stress-relieving devices such as hot drinks or chocolate. Just don't keep food or drink too near your paper!

You may have seen folders holding the paper in the air and making all the creases without resting on anything. These individuals are very experienced in origami and fold in this way so that others can

Amazing origami facts

Here's a list of things you never knew about origami – save these gems for dropping into conversation at elegant dinner parties.

✔ The word origami has only been in use in the English language for 50 years.

✔ You *can* fold a piece of paper in half more than seven times.

✔ You can solve quadratic and cubic equations by folding paper.

✔ The oldest known origami book, *Hiden Senbazuru Orikata*, was written in 1797.

✔ The largest origami crane was 65 metres by 36 metres. The smallest was folded from a 0.25 millimetre square piece of audio tape by Akira Naito.

✔ The simplest origami model has only one fold, the most complex more than 200 folds.

✔ There are more than 200 varieties of origami elephant.

✔ You can make origami models from food, metal, mesh, money, and of course, paper.

✔ Poppadom (People Out Practising Paperfolding and Dining on Masala) is a society dedicated to folding origami while eating curry.

✔ Saburo Kase both created and taught origami, despite being blind.

see what they're doing. In general though, it's best to fold on a flat surface, such as a table because neat, accurate creasing is a lot easier to achieve on a table.

This may seem like obvious advice, but remember to use both hands when folding. Your hands are a partnership in origami, with one holding the paper so it doesn't move, the other creasing it.

Try to alternate the hands that you hold and crease with so that it feels natural to make a crease with either hand. Readers blessed with three or more hands will have a distinct advantage when tackling modular origami.

Thinking first, creasing second!

Whenever and wherever you fold, you're always making creases. You need to put the crease in the right place at the first attempt because a crease that's been made in a sheet of paper can't be erased like a pencil line. The fibres of wood along the crease have been broken and can't be mended. Here's how to make a perfect crease:

1. Put the paper into position slowly, and take another few seconds to check the exact position of the layers or edges, checking the instructions as you do so.

2. When you're certain that everything's in order, hold the paper in place with one hand, freeing the other hand to make the crease. As with all matters dextrous, you can fold right- or left-handed, as you prefer.

3. Start the crease at the centre of the folded edge, using the pad of your finger to sweep out to first one side, then out to the other.

4. Once the crease is in place, put both fingers to the centre and run them outwards at the same time, to reinforce the crease. Think of your fingertips as an iron, putting a sharp crease into a shirt.

Don't start at one side and crease inwards, because you might 'ruffle' the paper, rucking it slightly like a badly fitted carpet. If you rush the process, you may have to make adjustments later on. Adjusted creases are far harder to work with and can make the finished model look sloppy.

As you progress in origami, you discover that creases don't all have to be made firmly. Sometimes a gentle or soft crease is more effective on a natural subject. Don't worry about this for now, I'll tell you when you might like to try making softer creases.

Patience is a virtue ... especially with origami

Patience is particular virtue worth having in the world of origami. You're bound to find a design that slightly (or greatly) exceeds your folding ability. Like any other skill, no real short-cuts exist; you simply have to persevere and give it time. Trying the most interesting and challenging projects first is always tempting, but not the best way to develop confidence.

Reading ahead

When you're following origami instructions, always look at the next step, so you have an idea of what you're trying to achieve.

At times you might work out how to make your paper match the next step without really knowing how. At that point, unfold the step and try to work out how the preceding drawing tried to get you there. Read the accompanying text as well; you may have missed an instruction in the text that isn't obvious from the drawing, such as which of several overlapping layers you may need to fold.

What to Fold With

You can get hold of so many different types of paper, it can be a confusing choice, but in this section I suggest some places to start. After a while, you'll be able to tell if paper is suitable simply by folding over the corner of a sheet. (If it isn't suitable, you unfold it and surreptitiously slip it back on the shelf.)

You can buy origami paper at most decent craft shops for around £2 per pack, depending on the type of paper. Origami paper usually comes in 6-inch squares, although you can buy both larger and smaller formats. For more complicated designs (such as those in Chapters 6 and 7), always fold from the largest convenient paper you have. If you need a rectangle other than of standard proportions, you'll probably need to cut it yourself.

Although paper is the obvious choice of folding material, you have many other alternatives, depending how strong you are and how much you enjoy a challenge!

 ✔ **Origami paper.** This paper is perfect for simple models, and a selection is included in this book. Origami paper comes in a huge variety of colour and pattern combinations, is usually perfectly square, and often very cheap. Each pack contains a selection of colours, although you can buy packs of a single colour (such as red, when Christmas approaches). This paper has a colour or pattern on one side and is plain white on the other.

✔ **Duo paper.** This paper has a different colour or pattern on each side.

✔ **Harmony paper.** This type of origami paper has patterns made of colours fading into each other. You won't see many experienced folders using it, because it's highly decorative and may distract from the lines of the model itself.

✔ **Foil paper.** One side of this paper is coloured foil, the other is white paper. This used to be highly popular, but the metallic finish isn't to everyone's taste, and it's almost impossible to reverse the direction of a crease.

✔ **Kraft paper.** Kraft paper is usually brown and comes in huge rolls for wrapping parcels. It's brilliant for folding and you can also find it in different colours, if you look around.

✔ **Canson.** A high quality art paper, canson is available in a variety of colours (the same both sides). It's ideal for larger models, especially if you're wet-folding (Chapter 9 explains wet-folding in more detail).

✔ **Elephant hide.** This paper isn't literally made from elephants, you'll be glad to hear! It has an elegant marbled effect, and is also good for wet-folding. Elephant hide is also known as Wyndstone paper.

✔ **Washi.** Washi is a Japanese word meaning 'handmade paper'. It's generally thicker than normal paper and requires some experience to fold with, but can produce outstanding results that last for many years.

✔ **Tracing paper.** You can fold with tracing paper, but it can be quite thick, making neat creases a little harder to achieve. However, tracing paper is great for bowls and vases.

✔ **Photocopy paper.** This is a cheap and widely-available material for folding with. It isn't very elegant and doesn't produce very sharp creases, but is perfect for practising and experimenting with. Photocopy paper is the material of choice for making paper planes!

✔ **Recycled paper.** Everyone gets more than enough junk mail through the letter-box, much of which you can fold into something or other – far better and greener than simply throwing it away.

✔ **Money.** Because it's designed to be hard-wearing, paper currency is great for folding. Pop into your nearest bank and ask what the cheapest form of paper currency is. You can then buy 100 fresh notes from an obscure country for a few pounds. When you give people origami gifts made from money, they think very highly of you! Whole books are devoted to the subject of models made from dollar bills.

✔ **Napkins.** A complete genre of origami is devoted to folding napkins, which are essentially big squares. Paper napkins are quite soft, so not every model will work. Waiters at up-market restaurants always know a few designs, or you could teach them new ones!

✔ **Cloth.** Origami techniques are widely used in the making of clothes, often in the form of pleats, but sometimes actually using origami bases. You can make models with towels (you may have seen *towelgami* creations left on your bed by the staff on cruise ships). You'll probably need to buy a large box of starch before starting.

✔ **Clay.** If you want a challenge, you can make thin sheets of clay and create simple designs before firing them. You need a kiln, which adds to the overall expense. A Japanese company has invented special ceramic paper for this purpose but, trust me, this requires a deft and damp touch!

✔ **Pastry.** You can use filo pastry and other forms of dough to fold with, so you can make your food look interesting even if it doesn't taste wonderful!

✔ **Sheet metal.** Some physically gifted folders have made designs from metal. Needless to say, don't try this if you have a delicate constitution. You can use thinner sheets of silver to make beautiful origami earrings and other jewellery.

✔ **Tea Bags.** Tea-bag folding originated in Holland and can produce geometric designs of great beauty. You actually fold the wrappers that the bags come in, although you could always try the bag itself.

✔ **Tickets.** Tickets for buses, trains, concerts, as well as general business cards are great for making simple designs, especially jumping frogs (Chapter 7 shows you how to make a jumping frog). Tickets are rarely square, so you should practise designs from rectangles.

✔ **Netting/Mesh.** You can get your hands on small squares of a type of thin mesh aimed specifically at origamists. The mesh produces a surprisingly attractive result if you make flowers using it.

Origami tools

All you really need to make origami models is paper and your hands (plus love, if you're a Beatles fan) but here are some tools that may enhance your folding experience. You can pick up these tools from most craft or art stores.

- ✔ **Folding tool.** A folding tool is a small strip with a rounded edge, a bit like a short chopstick. Traditionally made from bone, now plastic or wooden folding tools are widely available for a few pounds. Use them to *really* flatten creases. Some folders love them, others are more disdainful, Make up your own mind!

- ✔ **Trimmer.** An A3 rotary trimmer is perfect for preparing squares of the right size. Guillotine types are best for large sheets, but can be dangerous. If you decide to buy a trimmer, check that it cuts paper at right angles!

- ✔ **Paper storage.** Okay, storage isn't really a tool, but you need some means of storing paper to keep it flat and compact. Many suitable second-hand drawer units are out there, and you can use plastic wallets for smaller squares.

- ✔ **Model storage.** When you've made a superb model, you have four main choices about what to do with it. You can give it away (the altruistic option), display it (but most houses only have so much shelf space), throw it away (gasp), or store it. Smaller cardboard boxes that have been used for packaging are usually free from supermarkets. Put tissue paper, scrunched-up newspaper, or even polystyrene 'worms' in the box and arrange your model inside so it can't move about. The same applies in triplicate when you want to send origami through the post!

- ✔ **Cutting board and knife.** The knife isn't for cutting your models, but for preparing odd shaped paper, such as triangles or hexagons. Be *very* careful when cutting. I foolishly once cut on an old book resting on my knee, only to slide the knife off the end of the book and into my leg. Ouch.

- ✔ **Glue.** What? This is origami – no glue allowed, surely? Actually, glue is generally considered acceptable to use when preparing a model for display. You want it to stay in place under potentially adverse conditions and glue helps. Some folders use wet-folding techniques with liquid glue when folding intricate designs. The end result is as permanent as can be.

- ✔ **Digital camera.** A digital camera is perfect for making rough diagrams, keeping a gallery of your work, or capturing inspiring images from an exhibition. However, be aware that some folders don't allow their work to be photographed of fear of piracy. You can read more about making diagrams in Chapter 2.

- ✔ **Paper clips.** At times you'll wish you had extra hands, especially when assembling modular designs. A few well-placed paper clips can be really useful.

- ✔ **Hammer.** Sometimes layers of paper simply won't lie flat. You can use a small hammer to encourage the paper to do as it's told. Careful, now!

Not every design works with every medium, so experiment until the model works.

Knowing Your Symbols

At first glance, origami diagrams can appear a bit complicated, but once you master the basic symbols, they'll soon make perfect sense to you. You see about a dozen symbols on a regular basis, plus as many again that crop up less often. People who make lots of origami diagrams sometimes come up with their own variations and additions, but in general, origami diagrams from anywhere in the world use the same basic set:

> ✔ **Valley fold.** This is the fold everyone knows how to make – it's the one you use to fold a letter in half, for example. You fold the paper over and line up the edges (or corners), then use one hand to hold the paper in position and the other to iron in the crease, starting in the centre and working outwards. The symbol is a line with an arrow head of some kind at one end. A dashed line indicates where the crease should lie. The arrow gives you the direction in which to fold.

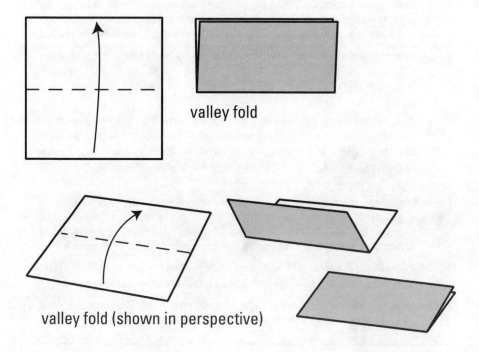

valley fold

valley fold (shown in perspective)

↙ **Valley and unfold.** Here you make a fold, then unfold it. This may form a reference crease to line up with, or you may refold it later on (they're then known as *precreases*). Different symbols are in common use but in this book I use the solid and hollow arrowheads – the solid arrowhead shows the direction to fold in, the hollow one shows where the fold returns to.

Why bother? I use this convention because for any given valley crease, you could fold paper from either side of the crease. In some cases it doesn't matter which way you fold (for example, a basic diagonal). In other cases, it's consider-ably *easier* to fold from a specific direction. Where there's no advantage to be gained from creasing in a certain direction, I use two solid arrowheads.

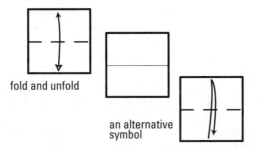

fold and unfold

an alternative
symbol

↙ **Existing crease.** When you've made a valley fold and unfolded the paper, it leaves a *crease line*, indicated by a very thin line. Crease lines are as important as edges of paper, because you use them to locate other folds.

↙ **Mountain fold.** This is the opposite of a valley fold because you fold the paper underneath. You either hold the paper in the air to fold, or turn the paper over and treat it as a valley fold, remembering to turn back over afterwards so you tally with the diagrams.

Every time you make a valley fold, you make a mountain fold on the opposite side of the paper. Strictly speaking, these are the only two types of creases you can make – all the others are combinations of mountains and valleys.

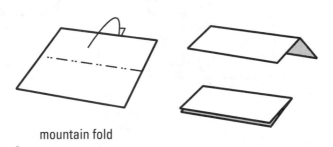

mountain fold

✔ **Unfold arrow.** The arrow line disappears behind an edge and then comes back. The unfold arrow is a solid white arrow showing that you're unfolding a layer, or easing paper out from between layers.

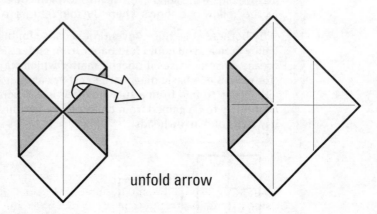

unfold arrow

✔ **Repeat arrow.** If a move is applied more than once, a repeat arrow means 'do the same'. If a folding line has a small line (or lines) across it, you repeat the indicated fold somewhere – it's usually obvious where, but the text should make it clear, or you can check the next drawing. If a fold line has three lines on it, you repeat the action three times, for example when folding all four corners into the centre.

The repeat arrow is used for one of two reasons: to keep the instructions simple and easy to follow, or because the artist is too lazy to draw the sequence over and over again.

The repeat arrow is also used to indicate repeating a sequence of steps, in which case it has the number of the first and last steps to be repeated alongside.

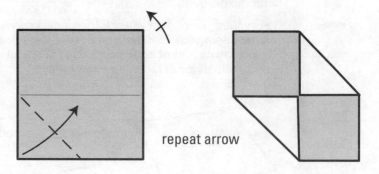

repeat arrow

✔ **Fold Point to Point.** A small circle helps to show which part of the paper meets which other point. Make sure you can locate both points before proceeding!

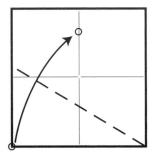 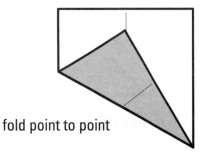

fold point to point

✔ **Turn the paper over.** Pick the paper up and turn it over. The paper is turned in the direction of the symbol, generally from side to side like turning the pages of a book, but sometimes from top to bottom (or vice versa) as if you were tossing a pancake.

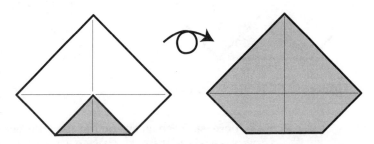

✔ **Rotate the paper.** Sometimes, you need to rotate the paper relative to the previous step. This could be 180 degrees or perhaps 90 degrees. The symbol makes clear which way to turn and by how much.

I use the 90-degree symbol flexibly to indicate some kind of rotation that's less or equal to 90 degrees. Because folds are most easily made away from your body on a horizontal axis, turning the paper can make a diagonal fold much easier.

Look carefully at the rotate symbol – rotating a hexagon through 30 degrees can be a subtle change and can lead to unwanted creasing if you don't spot it.

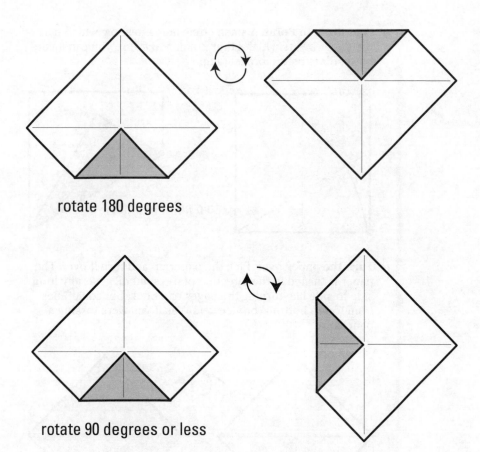

rotate 180 degrees

rotate 90 degrees or less

✔ **Scale increase.** Keep an eye out for the little 'scale increases' arrow, used where the next drawing is shown larger than it would be in reality to makes it easier to read. The symbol doesn't tell you to do anything, but provides information. Sometimes you'll see a matching 'scale decreases' symbol.

scale increases

✔ **Press or apply pressure.** A small black triangle means you need to apply some pressure in a given direction. Nothing too excessive is required, just gentle pressure. The triangle is also used to show in which direction to move the paper (often used in reverse folds – coming up!).

apply pressure

✔ **New viewpoint.** The eye shows you where the next step is viewed from.

new viewpoint

✔ **Outside reverse fold.** With an outside reverse, both layers wrap around on opposite sides, to the outside. You can make these easier by *pre-creasing* – making the indicated crease as an ordinary valley fold through all layers, then unfolding.

The key to reverse folds is to make the pre-crease a firm one. Pre-creasing always puts in the creases you need, but some of them always need swapping from valley to mountain or vice-versa. You have to do a *bit* of work.

1. Start with a square folded in half on a diagonal. Fold the top corner to the bottom corner, crease firmly, and unfold.

2. Change the crease on this side of the paper to a mountain and carefully start to manoeuvre the paper in-between the layers.

3. Here's the move in progress.

4. And completed.

The Duck sequence in Chapter 2 is a good model to try out an outside reverse fold.

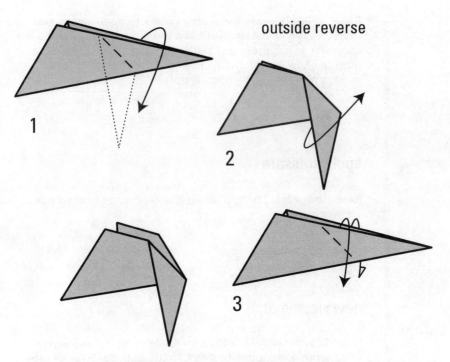

outside reverse

✔ **Inside reverse fold.** Pre-crease the paper like you did for the outside reverse fold, then turn the creases on both sides into a mountain crease, gently pressing the paper up and in-between the original layers. The black triangle indicates the direction in which to apply pressure.

To put this fold in action, make the Miniphant model in Chapter 4.

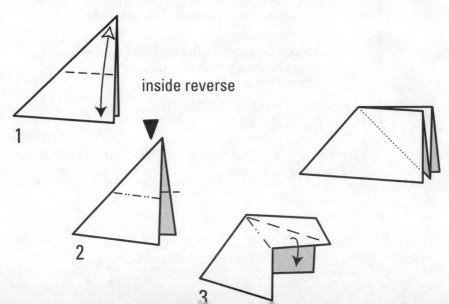

inside reverse

✔ **Double reverse fold.** If you make an inside, then an outside reverse fold, you can create heads or beaks

✔ **X-ray view.** Dotted lines indicate the hidden flaps, to give an idea of what's going on in between the layers.

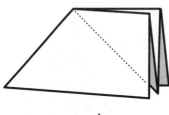

x-ray view

✔ **Inside crimp.** Pre-crease both indicated creases through both layers, then make them valley and mountain on both sides. The paper acts like a hinge. This is often used when forming heads.

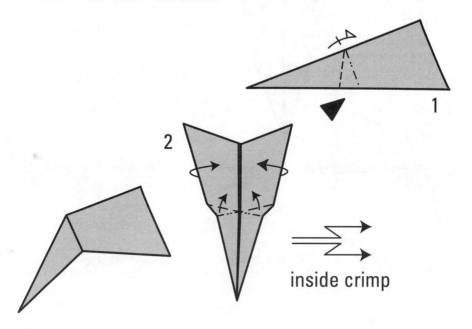

inside crimp

✔ **Outside crimp.** A similar move to the inside crimp, but the paper swivels on the outside, rather than the inside. You simply need to make the mountain and valley creases in the correct order.

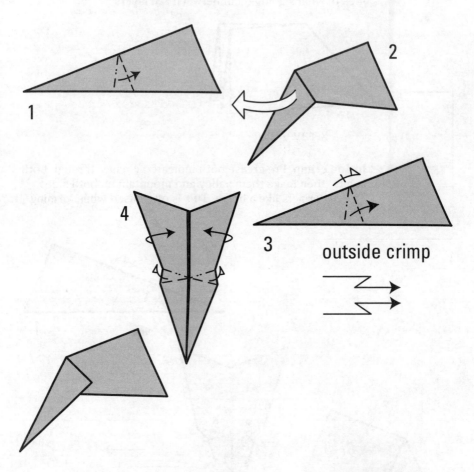

outside crimp

✔ **Squash.** A squash fold is a satisfying move where you pre-crease all the creases, then apply a bit of pressure to gain the required result.

1. Fold a square in half from top to bottom.

2. Crease in half from side to side.

3. Fold the top left corner to the lower centre. Note the hollow arrowhead shows where to *start* the fold. Crease and unfold.

4. Lift the left half of the paper up at 90 degrees. The right-angle symbol clarifies this.

5. Put one finger in between the upright layers and start to press on the vertical spine. The idea is to persuade both diagonal creases to be mountains from the outside. One already is, and the other needs persuading to change direction.

6. This is the move in progress.

7. The squash is complete.

squash

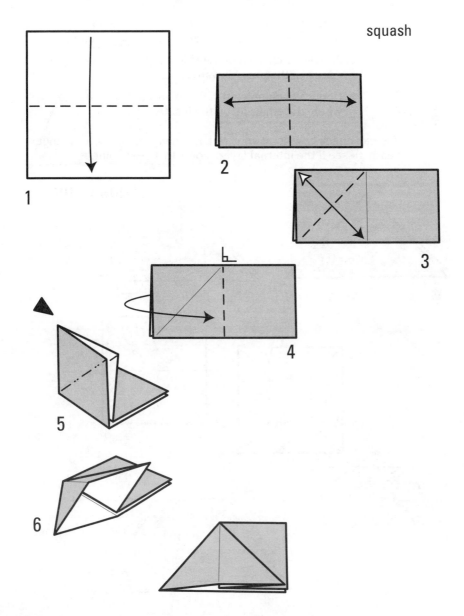

✔ **Sink.** The sink is a descriptive name for when a *closed* corner is folded back inside itself. By closed, I mean with no raw edges.

1. Here's a sink in a single step. The next steps break it down.

2. Make a firm valley fold to indicate where the sink will take place, then unfold back to the square.

3. Where necessary, alter the creases that form the central square so that they're all valley creases.

4. Partially form the creases shown, turning the paper over to outline the central square, almost like a table-top.

5. As you pinch each of the sides together, encourage the centre of the paper inwards.

6. Here's the completed sink. The dotted lines shown where the edges lie on the inside.

You can check how good your sink is by having a peek from underneath, to see if the internal layers come to a neat point.

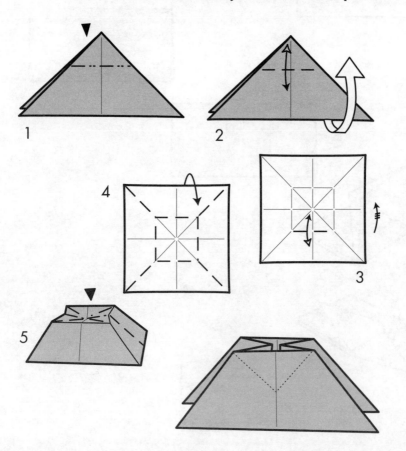

↙ **Rabbit ear.** This move is widely used in origami.

1. Start with a square creased along both diagonals. Fold the lower left edge to the horizontal centre, creasing only as far as the vertical diagonal.

2. Repeat the fold on the right.

3. Fold both sides in at the same time, using the creases shown. A small pointed flap forms in the centre.

4. Flatten the flap to the right.

5. The completed rabbit's ear.

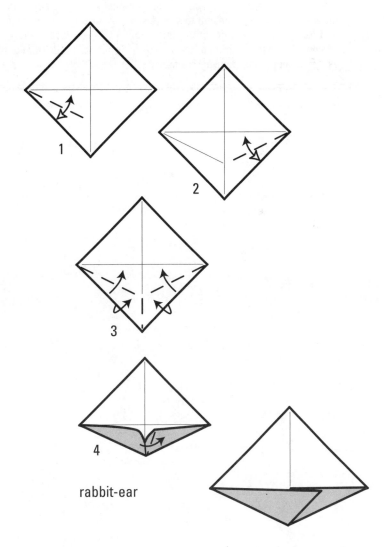

rabbit-ear

The history of origami symbols

In the earliest days of origami, no coherent system for creating instructions existed. Even well into the 20th century a variety of symbols were used to show how to fold – no wonder that origami remained a relatively obscure activity for so long.

In the early 1950s a Japanese origami master called Akira Yoshizawa published his first book, using a system of dotted lines and arrows he'd developed in order to diagram his paper creations. A South African man called Robert Harbin, wrote a book called *Paper Magic* in 1956. In it, he presented certain common sequences and gave them names, such as 'squash fold', and 'crimp fold'. He also collaborated with an American called Sam Randlett to create symbols for origami diagrams. These differed from, but were undoubtedly influenced by those of Yoshizawa. With some additions, the symbols from this very international collection of men remains the basis of all modern origami diagrams.

Chapter 2

Drawing Diagrams and Getting Creative

*A*fter making the models in this book, I hope you'll want to turn your hand to creating your own models, and diagramming them to share with other origamists. Diagrams are simply a means to communicate how to fold an origami model. Diagrams range from rough hand-drawn scribbles through to computer generated works of art. In this chapter I cover the many different ways you can create diagrams, depending on much time and enthusiasm you have!

Creating models isn't for everybody; probably the majority of origamists have never created a single new model, perhaps thinking it's beyond them. In this chapter I show you ways of approaching the creative challenge! I also touch upon the issue of origami 'ethics', an important topic in continuing to develop the art of origami around the world.

Drawing Diagrams

Reasons abound why it's a good idea to try your hand at making diagrams, even if you didn't create the model in question. Perhaps the most important is so that you can fold a model again and not rely on your memory. Very few people are blessed with photographic origami memories and you can quickly forget a folding sequence without some visual aid. And while thousands of origami diagrams are in books, newer or obscure models may not have been diagrammed and are passed on from person to person.

Preparing diagrams also helps you to really get to grips with a model, as you fold and unfold in search of the best sequence. By the time you've finished, the model will be much more firmly stored in your memory. If the design is one of your own, diagrams enable you to share the fold with others. Sharing diagrams is fundamental to origami – if we didn't share models with each other, the hobby would never have taken off as it has. (Remember to ask the creator before sharing a diagram.)

Always assume that the reader won't be an expert, so use as many steps as the model needs – don't be tempted to take diagramming short-cuts.

You might look at the artwork in books like this and think 'I could never do anything as good as this', but neither could I when I started and look what Dali-esque masterpieces I'm churning out now! My first hundred or so diagrams were drawn by hand, amply demonstrating my complete lack of natural artistic skills, training, or understanding of perspective. Check out the step from an early 'sheep skull' design in Figure 2-1 – so good that I haven't folded it in twenty years. Despite all this, I kept at it.

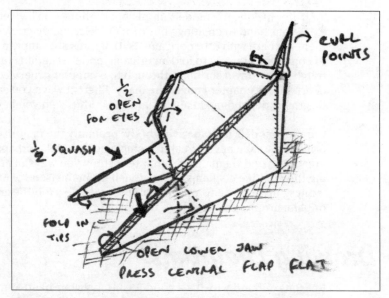

Figure 2-1: My early sheep skull design.

Using a computer enabled me to make huge leaps in the standard of my output. Perhaps most importantly I can now easily arrange the drawings and text on the page, as the layout of diagrams is very important.

When diagramming, consider:

- ✔ **Symbols.** Use the internationally recognised symbol set (explained in Chapter 1) and avoid the more obscure ones, unless they make things substantially clearer. Don't be tempted to invent your own symbols.

  If you use a computer, build up a library file of common symbols. This saves lots of time and adds consistency to your diagrams.

- ✔ **Line width.** The paper edge should be the thickest line in your diagrams. Existing creases are much thinner lines that stop just short of the paper's edge. Valley and mountain lines are somewhere in between. Use consistent widths.

- ✔ **3D steps.** Few people have the ability to draw accurately in three dimensions. One solution is to photograph the model, import the photo into your drawing package and use it as a guide before deleting it (or even leaving the photo in place if you prefer).

Making rough sketches

The most low-tech method of diagramming is to make a series of rough sketches as shown in Figure 2-2.

Take a large sheet of paper to fold with, a white rectangle for your diagram, a pencil, and (just in case) an eraser. Follow these steps.

1. Draw a square.

2. Make a fold and unfold it.

3. Draw the fold as a valley or mountain, with an arrow.

4. Write the number 1 next to it.

5. Refold the step.

6. Draw the paper as it is now.

7. Repeat step 2 with the next fold.

If you feel that a step needs more clarification, add a few words underneath. If the drawing is wrong, erase and redraw it. Remember, your diagram doesn't have to be a work of art. Your drawn squares don't need to be square, nor your lines straight, although make them as accurate as you can manage. Some people draw on graph paper to help keep things neater.

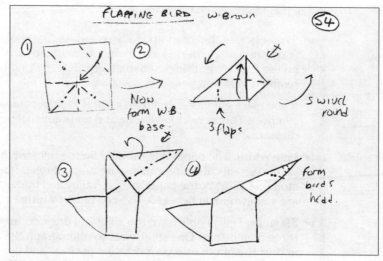

Figure 2-2: Making simple diagrams.

Taking photographs

Since the advent of the cheap digital camera, everyone has access to digital images and what a fabulous thing they are! Instead of drawing each step, you can photograph it. You can print out so many photos per page, and add fold lines, text, or whatever else you need.

You can either get close to the paper so it fills the camera screen (you may need to use 'macro' mode on your camera) or shoot normally and crop the image using image software. The advantage of this method is that it shows 3D moves far more easily than drawing can and is also quicker. Figure 2-3 shows three typical photo steps from an origami box – not perfect examples of photography, but enough for our purposes.

Figure 2-3: Photo steps – crude but adequate!

Be inspired

Look closely at other people's diagrams. Find a style that you like and try to copy it. Look at the way the artist indicates layers, or uses shade. If you make enough diagrams and think carefully about what you're doing, you'll eventually develop a style of your own. Hand-drawn diagrams naturally have a life of their own, but there's no reason why you can't add some personality to computer diagrams such as adding curves to paper edges, 3D shading, and artistic line styles with varying thicknesses along their length. The more attractive your diagrams are, the more inspired people will be to fold from them!

Using drawing software

If you have a computer and are prepared to put some learning time in, the best solution for diagrams is to use a drawing package. The vast majority of serious diagrammers all use computer software. Don't be tempted to try a computer-aided design or paint package; *vector drawing* (where you create lines by clicking and dragging) is most appropriate here. Luckily you don't need the high-end software – origami drawings generally only use a small fraction of the software's potential. If you can afford Adobe or Macromedia products, that's fine, but many shareware or trial versions are available on the Internet that do a perfectly adequate job.

The advantages of drawing software are many and varied. Many origami steps are closely related to the previous one, so you can copy and paste steps, making whatever alterations you need to. You can save and reuse symbols and bases freely, reducing your drawing time. You can zoom in to make fine changes easily, and use grids to snap to for outlining shapes quickly. You can enlarge or reduce steps to produce your perfect layout. You can easily use shade or colour to indicate the coloured side of the paper.

If you're feeling adventurous you can also use flash technology to create animated diagrams. Derek Stancombe in the UK is one of the leaders in this field, and you can see his excellent work, along with tutorials, at www.origami.org.uk.

Reverse engineering

Reverse engineering is a process you can use to discover how to fold and diagram a model when all you have is the completed design. This method requires practice and patience, but does work if you have no other options and if the model doesn't have 300 steps. Here's how:

1. Sketch or photograph the finished model.
2. Find the most obvious fold, and unfold and refold many times until you're certain how it works. Leave unfolded.
3. Sketch or photograph the model.
4. Repeat until you get back to the square of paper.

If you then reverse the order of the photos or drawings, you have a method to follow. Fold the model *immediately* to test your efforts, revising them accordingly. Throughout the process, don't alter any creases; keep the paper loose and let the creases remember their orientation wherever possible.

Crease patterns

Some folders can reproduce a model using the unfolded crease pattern only. This is the pattern of creases revealed when you unfold a base or finished model back to the square of paper. However, this is a skilled task and not for beginners, so it's a diagramming method used only by more experienced folders.

Figure 2-4 shows the crease patterns for the classic bases explained in Chapter 3. They show the basic creases you need to fold each base, even though the standard process of folding it might introduce some extra creases. In the kite base pattern, I've shaded a specific area consisting of a triangle with a crease in it. You can see in the fish base that the same area is reproduced four times, eight times in the bird base, and sixteen times in the frog base. The shaded area in the preliminary and waterbomb bases (which share the same crease pattern) can be seen multiplied eight times within the blintz base and sixteen times in the multiform base.

A central concept to origami is that you can break down complex patterns into combinations of simple patterns. What may look like a fiendishly complicated end result is often comprised of techniques you'd find in much simpler designs.

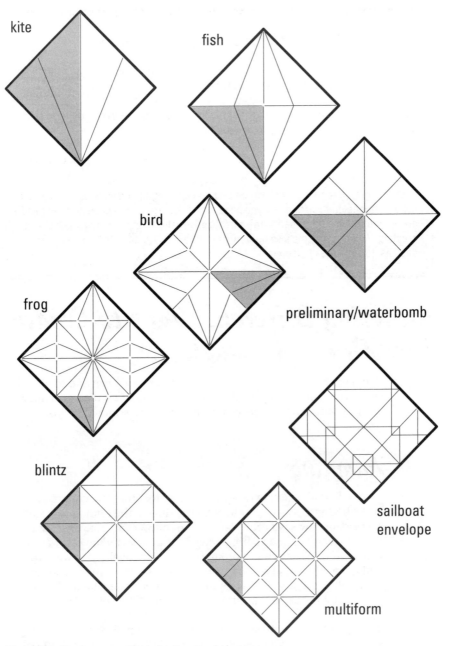

kite

fish

bird

preliminary/waterbomb

frog

blintz

sailboat envelope

multiform

Figure 2-4: The crease patterns for the classic bases.

Lighting the creative spark

If you're happy folding other people's work and have no desire to create original origami designs, that's absolutely fine. Everyone reads books, but not many people want to write one! However, I meet many folders who say 'I'm just not creative' and allow that single idea to hold them back. I firmly believe that everyone has talent and potential. The lucky ones discover what that talent is and pursue it. The vast majority simply never find out what they're good at, either through lack of encouragement, shyness, lack of opportunity, or most likely, a simple matter of chance – life works that way.

I encourage you to try as many varied and unusual (legal) activities as you can, on the off-chance that you find one you have a gift for. I urge you to have an open mind about whether you have 'patience', 'talent', or 'artistic ability', and just have a go at creating. When you try the introductory designs in Chapters 2 and 4, you realise that designs don't have to be complex!

Exploring Different Ways to Create New Origami Models

You have many different approaches to creating origami to choose from. You can use any or all of them, or none if you have an alternative approach that works for you. Here are some ideas you can try.

Adapting

As you fold an existing design, you may feel that the end result looks better if you alter things a little during the folding sequence. No origami law says that you have to follow diagrams exactly, or that you can't turn an African elephant into an Indian elephant if you want to. What you're doing is being creative! If you want to fold a blackbird and someone else has designed a pigeon, study your subject and see what changes you need to make to the pigeon sequence in order to capture the characteristics of a blackbird.

Making subtle alterations to an existing design is good fun, but strictly speaking, you're not creating original work. If you choose to diagram or exhibit your adaptation, make sure you credit your sources. If you want to publish the model, make sure the creator of the original work gives approval. There comes a point where you adapt something so radically that it crosses the border into originality. Exactly where this happens is impossible to quantify, but be honest and don't try to pass off others' work as your own.

Doodling

This highly unscientific approach involves playing with the paper until you can see a possible subject emerging, which you can then consciously develop and refine. Try to use your imagination to find the subject that's trying to break free from the paper. Doodling is like seeing faces in clouds – once you've spotted the basic shape, your mind fills in the missing details.

A firm grasp of origami techniques is very helpful for when you decide that a given flap needs to become a tail, or develop claws. If you're trying to create an animal or bird, you may want to start with an existing base that gives suitable flaps to start with. You probably won't develop an original and appropriate base until you're a really experienced folder.

Planning ahead

More experienced folders are able to choose a subject and work towards a base that provides flaps in the right places. This method is generally for more advanced creators who have plenty of folding experience. If you decide to create an origami Ford Model T car, break it down into the elements that you really want. Will the car be 2D or 3D? If you want wheels, how are you going to make them? How much paper do you need? These are the types of questions you'll face.

Is it original?

At first you'll probably rediscover designs that other creators have found before you when you start to create. This isn't a problem! It's only natural that you want your work to be original, but equally probable that others, given the same circumstances and experience, may follow similar creative paths, even on relatively complex designs. Take heart, because every time you come up with a new design, however heavily influenced or adapted, you're learning things and taking one more step towards truly original work.

Keep your rejects!

Treat yourself to a large cardboard box and label it Potential Classics. Whenever you come up with anything that has potential, even a single interesting technique, store it in the box for a rainy day. Some creations reach fruition quickly, others need time to ferment in the back of your mind. The project that you couldn't finish today may develop significantly if you try it again in a few weeks time.

For example, when she heard I was writing this book, my origami friend Rachel Katz suggested including a dunce's cap in Chapter 4. Take a look at that design while I explain the thinking behind it.

Needing a narrow triangular shape, I started with a kite base, folding the triangular flap over for the base of the cap. Re-arranging the flaps allowed me to 'lock' the paper together but the shape was too narrow and asymmetrical. So I decided to enlarge the angle to 30 degrees.

This geometry had the additional bonus that the layers overlapped perfectly, because the angle is exactly one third of the corner of a square. So now I had the upper part of the cap, but now needed to tuck away the paper at the lower end, so that the cap held together properly and had a horizontal base. I tried mountain folding the lower section inside but it required extra creases and didn't seem like a good solution.

The main part of the cap was rather flimsy, so I tried doubling up the layers by folding the paper on a diagonal (after placing the 30 degree creases in place). This gave the cap more bulk and turning over, gave a good location for the horizontal crease. The next step seemed too good not to use, folding the edges around the sides of the cap to enable the lower section to fit perfectly into the 'pocket'.

Creating in origami throws up plenty of problems and solving even a few gives you a warm glow inside. You *can* be creative!

Avoiding the obvious

The more your origami horizons widen, the better your knowledge of existing designs will be. You quickly realise that making a penguin from a kite base or a bird from a bird base is unlikely to be very original. Likewise, subjects such as elephants and pandas are very popular, so why not choose less common subjects that share similar features, such as the anteater or the badger? Innovative work often comes from deliberately avoiding accepted practices.

Understanding Origami Ethics

Throughout this book, I remind you to credit inspiration where due. Origami ethics are becoming more and more relevant in today's 'file-sharing' era where many people assume that if something can be downloaded, it must be in the public domain. One result of ignoring creators' rights is that creators become more restrictive in how they share their work, to the great loss of all true origami fans.

By the way, my opinions in this section (although widely shared) *don't* constitute legal advice but please heed them anyway!

Copyright

Copyright is an issue of increasing importance to origami designers, as well as authors and professionals who use origami to earn a living. In the good old days, origami was an obscure art and the only issue that really mattered was who came first. Authors from within origami were generally respectful of a model's ownership, but some people felt at liberty to help themselves to designs, treating every model as if it were traditional. The Internet makes scanning diagrams and publishing (or even selling!) them online very easy.

There are precious few legal precedents to establish exactly what you can and can't do with origami designs, but in general, there are no restrictions on folding or displaying a model in a non-commercial way. If you want to sell origami, or fold it for money, you must either use your own creations, or seek permission from the creator.

Few people would quibble about making a diagram of someone else's work for your own personal use, but that doesn't mean you can distribute it freely. You can do as you please with your own design – many creators publish their models on the Internet for others to enjoy. You may be unlucky enough to find that someone else created an almost identical model before you, but providing that you didn't knowingly copy it, you should be OK. In the end, it's a matter for your conscience.

If you want to delve deeper into the legal aspect of all this, take a look at *Patents, Copyright, Trademarks, and Registered Design For Dummies* by Henri Charmasson, John Grant, and Charlie Ashworth (Wiley).

Selling

Many websites sell folded examples of origami without the creator being consulted or paid for their efforts. It's almost impossible for the designer to pursue international legal action due to difficulties with language, legal procedure, and the expense. If you see origami for sale, ask the vendor about the ownership. Ultimately, the only accurate information comes from the original creator, so if you unwittingly buy something you find to be suspect, let the creator know. If you want to sell origami, *always* contact the creator first.

E-books

The ease with which some people can harvest designs and sell them online makes the temptation for easy money too much to resist. Some sites even offer scans of entire books, in clear breach of any accepted copyright principles. Preventing these pages from appearing on pirate sites is hard, but some even show up on more legitimate sites. Challenge anyone who breaches copyright, anyone who abuses the trust and generosity of origami designers, and anyone who profits illegally from the work of others. As a folder and now part of the origami community, you can help to police this. Firstly, just email the person and ask for an explanation, then contact the original creator or an origami society and pass the information on to them.

Part II
Folding On:
The Models

The 5th Wave — By Rich Tennant

BILLY HAD A HARD TIME APPRECIATING HIS FATHER'S INTEREST IN INDUSTRIAL ORIGAMI

"Why, that's an R—404L hydraulic hose crimper, Billy. Look, you can even see the integrated backup ring."

In this part . . .

It's time to roll up your sleeves, flex your fingers, and prepare to delve into making origami models. The chapters in this part start easy and become more difficult, so I suggest you don't dive into Chapter 7 right away (although your enthusiasm is commendable).

The chapters in this part are teeming with animals, birds, fish, and insects. You can make bowls, vases, and hats. You'll also find stars, flowers, tessellations, and geometric models.

I hope you thoroughly enjoy making the models in this part.

Chapter 3

Making Bases and Dividing the Paper

*Y*ou see several short sequences again and again in different models. These are known as *bases* (older books may call them *foundation folds*) and they're worth learning by name, so if someone says 'make a waterbomb base, colour outside', you can make the next few folds without instruction. Dividing paper into equal sections is another essential skill you'll need to perfect.

Kite Base

The kite is the simplest origami base, made by folding two sides in to meet a diagonal:

1. Start with a square, white side up, turned so a corner is nearest to you. Fold in half from side to side, crease und unfold.

2. Fold left and right lower edges to the centre crease.

3. This is the kite base. I wonder where the name came from?

Despite its simplicity, you can use the kite base to create many models.

To practise making the kite base, have a go at making the Duck model on the next page.

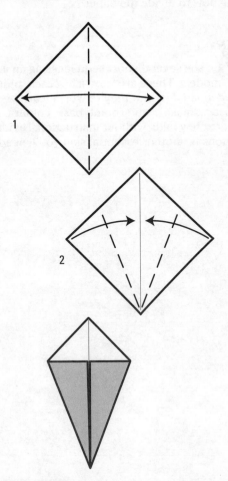

Duck

This is a traditional model that I've varied a bit.

1. Start with a kite base and turn the paper over.

2. Fold in half from left to right.

3. Rotate the paper clockwise. Fold the narrow point to match the dotted lines. Crease firmly and unfold.

4. Open the paper slightly and make sure your creases match this pattern (you have to change one from mountain to valley, and change the diagonal partly to a valley.)

5. This shows the reverse in progress.

6. This is the reverse completed. Form the head by folding over the tip to match the dotted lines. Crease firmly and unfold.

7. Make an outside reverse fold as you did in the previous three steps.

8. Here's the first option; the simplest duck. If you feel ambitious, carry on; if not, skip it and try again later.

9. Unfold the body from the bottom upwards.

10. Fold two edges to the centre crease.

11. Fold the upper section back down.

12. Here's option two; a more slender duck. Again, rest or continue!

13. Fold the rear (circled) corner to the opposite corner.

14. Leave a small gap, then fold it back.

15. Fold the upper section back down.

16. Hold where circled with two hands. Gently rotate the rear end out and up. The movement happens around where the dart indicates.

17. Fold the sides of the tail in as you did in step 14.

18. This is the third and most sophisticated duck (visually speaking!).

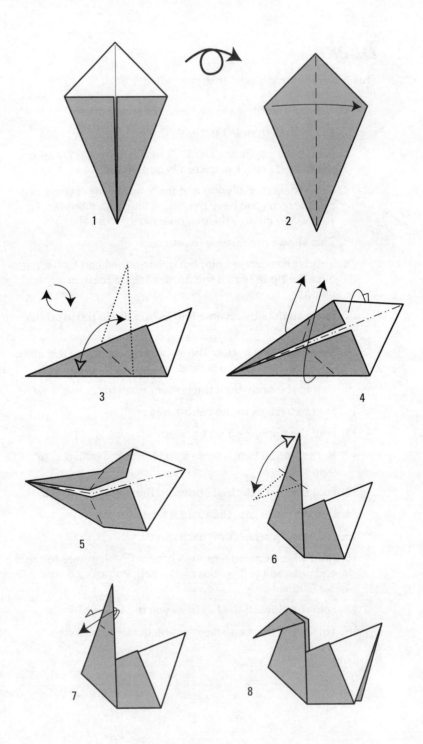

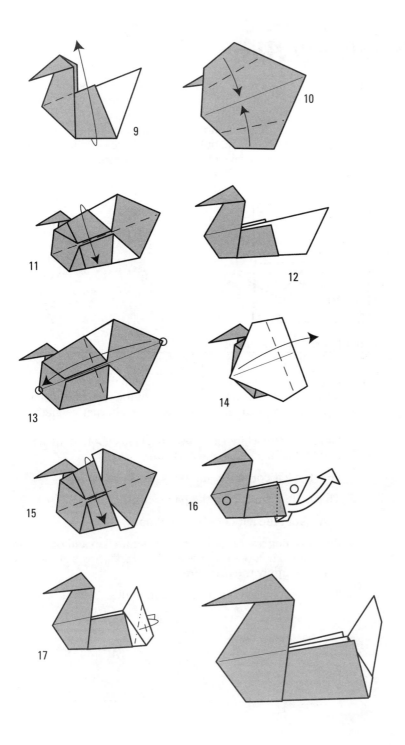

Waterbomb Base

Figure 3-1 shows the crease pattern you need for the waterbomb base, sometimes called a 'Union Jack' crease pattern. Note how the diagonals are valley folds and the side to side crease (otherwise known as a *book fold*) is a mountain. You actually need just three creases to collapse the base, but the vertical crease is almost certainly needed, so you always put it in for this base.

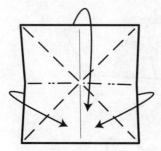

Figure 3-1: The crease pattern for the waterbomb base.

You may be surprised to discover that you can make the same base in a totally different way. This is one of the joys of origami – you have several ways to fold a cat. Here's an alternative method:

1. Start with the white side upwards, crease both diagonals, and fold in half using one of them.

2. Fold the left corner to the top.

3. This is the result. Turn the paper over.

4. Again, fold the left corner to the top.

5. Put your fingers inside the central white flap and open out, pressing in half the other way. The black arrows show where to apply the pressure.

6. The waterbomb, via a different method!

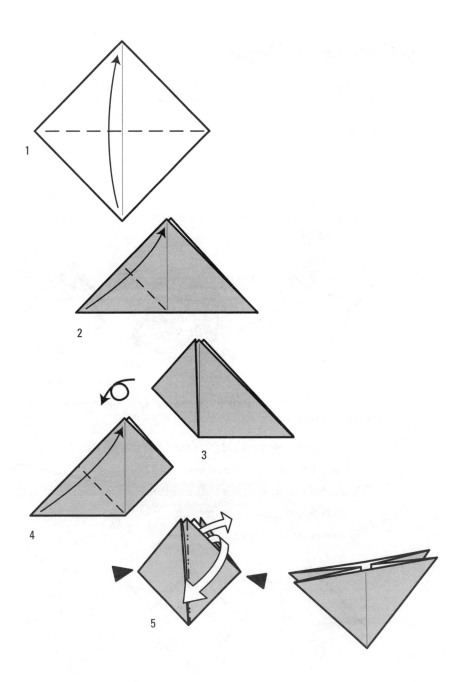

Preliminary Base

I hope that you'll be pleasantly surprised to discover that you already know how to make this base. The preliminary base is in fact the waterbomb base turned inside out, using exactly the same creases. Here are the steps to prove it:

1. Open out the waterbomb base and press gently in the centre.

2. Keep pressing until it pops inside out to this position.

3. Bring the corners together using the existing creases. This is a preliminary base.

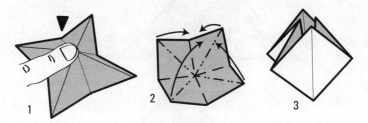

You can use similar methods to the waterbomb base. Here's how we make a preliminary with the colour outside.

1. Coloured side upwards, crease both diagonals.

2. Turn the paper over and book-fold both ways.

3. Fold the wide corners to the bottom, collapsing the paper.

4. This is the move in progress.

5. The complete preliminary base.

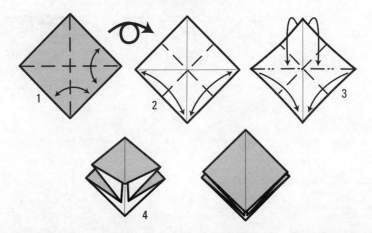

The Blintz Base

The blintz is one of the easiest bases around, reputedly named after a Jewish pastry made by folding four corners to the centre. In order to achieve this using paper, you need to know where the centre is. You can either book fold in half twice, fold both diagonals, or use some combination of the two. The method I prefer is to fold the paper in half, then fold to the edge instead of the crease. Here's what I mean:

1. Start with a square, coloured side upwards. Book-fold in half downwards.

2. Fold the outer edges to the top edge.

3. This is the result. Turn the paper over.

4. Repeat step 3.

5. Unfold the lower layer upwards from underneath.

6. The blintz base.

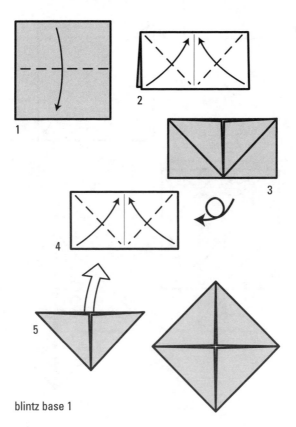

blintz base 1

Here's the minimal crease method:

1. Start with a square, white side upwards. Pinch the centre section of a diagonal.

2. Repeat with the other diagonal.

3. Fold the corners in to the centre.

4. Complete.

You can try out the blintz base on the Bluebell model in Chapter 5 and you can make a blintzed fish base in the Dragon model in Chapter 7.

alternate blintz base

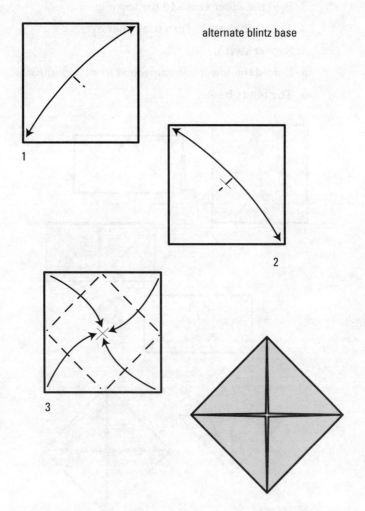

Fish Base

Both the waterbomb and preliminary bases need a minimum of three creases; the fish base needs at least five. I say 'at least' because you can fold any given base in different ways, some more efficient, some easier for the beginner. Here's the easy way:

1. Start with a square, white side up, turned so a corner is nearest to you. Crease and unfold both diagonals.

2. Fold left and right lower edges to the centre crease.

3. You probably recognise this as the kite base. Turn the paper over.

4. Fold the lower corner to the top corner. Turn the paper over.

5. Put your finger inside the pocket on the left and ease out the corner. At the same time, fold the upper left edge to lie on the vertical centre crease.

6. This is the result.

7. Repeat step 5 on the right-hand side.

8. Your fish base is complete.

Notice that the base has a familiar kite shape, but you have many more possibilities due to the extra layers. Unfold the base back to a square and you'll see that the creases made in step 2 extend all the way to the edge. You might decide to make the creases *only* as far as they needed to be, and then collapse the base. This is perhaps not very elegant, but has no surplus creases – try it out with the Fish Base Mask.

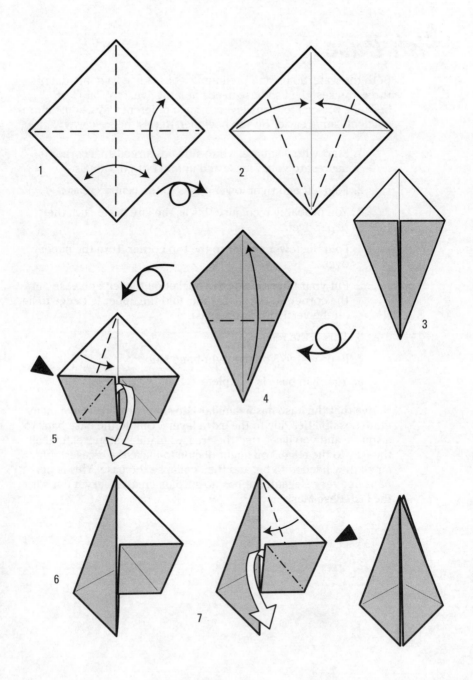

Nick's Fish Base Mask

Many simple designs are only slight variations on a base. Here's a mask that uses the basic creases of the fish base to good effect.

1. Start with a square, white side up, turned so a corner is nearest to you. Crease and unfold both diagonals.

2. Fold each edge to the nearest diagonal, but crease only as far as the vertical diagonal.

3. Repeat this on the other three sides.

4. Here's the crease pattern so far. Try to fold the fish base from here without adding any extra creases.

5. Carrying on, turn the paper over and fold a crease that passes through the lower intersections of the creases. Unfortunately, there's no location to fold *to*, so fold carefully and don't flatten the paper until you're certain the crease passes through the proper place. You'll meet this method again.

6. Repeat step 5 on the upper half.

7. Now collapse the base almost like a fish base, but forming a diamond-shaped central section.

8. Fold the narrow flaps to meet each other, opening the paper along the vertical centre crease. You're not (intentionally) making any new creases at this stage.

9. Fold the upper flap upwards so the corner lies on the vertical centre. Note the dash on the fold arrow, meaning you need to repeat this step on the underside as well.

10. Fold the small triangular section over and underneath the layer on the right. Repeat on the underside.

11. Open out the layers carefully.

12. You should see something like this!

If you don't get the desired result, play with the paper for a while to see if you can see the problem, then fold it again from scratch. Each time you fold the model, it'll be neater and you'll get closer to completing it.

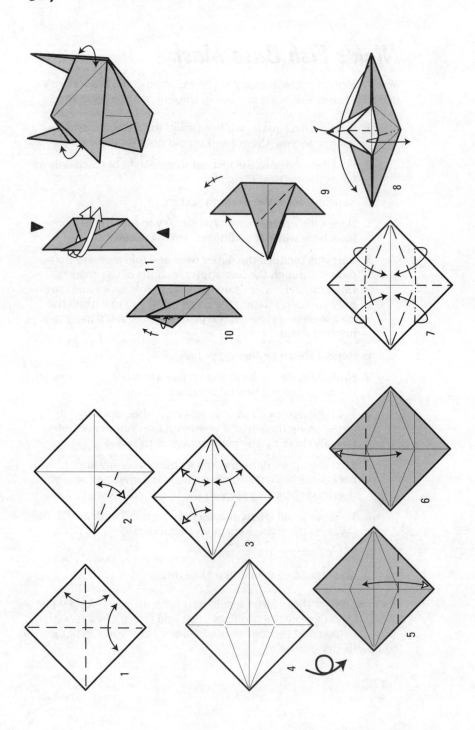

Bird Base

The bird base is one of the most popular bases and is used to create many models apart from a bird! This base is a masterpiece of elegance and economy – after making it, unfold it to see how perfectly arranged the creases are. The bird base is a progression from the simpler preliminary base.

The move between steps 8 and 10 is known as a *petal fold* and occurs quite often in origami.

1. Start with a square, coloured side upwards. Crease both diagonals and turn the paper over.

2. Book fold in half both ways.

3. Rotate the paper slightly and use the existing creases to collapse the paper into a preliminary base.

4. Fold the first pairs of raw edges on the left to meet the vertical centre.

5. Repeat on the right.

6. Fold the triangular flap at the top downwards.

7. Unfold the two flaps underneath the triangular flap.

8. Lift up a single layer on either side and ease it upwards. The paper hinges on the horizontal upper edge.

9. Here's the move in progress.

10. And complete.

11. Repeat steps 4 to 9 on the underside.

12. Here's the bird base in the raised position. Fold down upper and lower flaps from the top.

13. This is the normal configuration of the bird base.

Here's another way of getting the same result. This method uses reverses and avoids a horizontal crease:

1. Start with a preliminary base and fold both double edges to the vertical centre. Crease and unfold, and repeat underneath.

2. Inside reverse the two corners on the front and back.

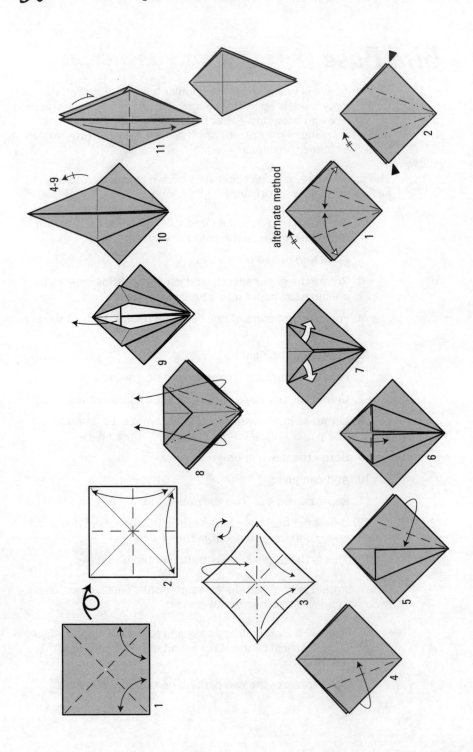

Putting wind beneath the wings

Here's a neat trick you can do with the bird base, discovered by Takuji Sigimura of Japan. It exploits the symmetry of the base by enabling you to perform a continuous rotation of the flaps. The creases need breaking in for a short while, but then the model should move smoothly. This trick is a great way both to practise this base and to get used to handling the paper gently but firmly.

1. Start with the bird base, holding it by the lower flaps. Ease them away from each other, at the same time encouraging the upper flaps to fold downwards.

2. Here's the halfway point – the upper flaps have folded down and begin to fold in half down the centre. The lower flaps are moving upwards.

3. Continue the action.

4. You should end up where you started, with the paper rotated by 90 degrees. Repeat for twenty minutes to develop your flapping muscles!

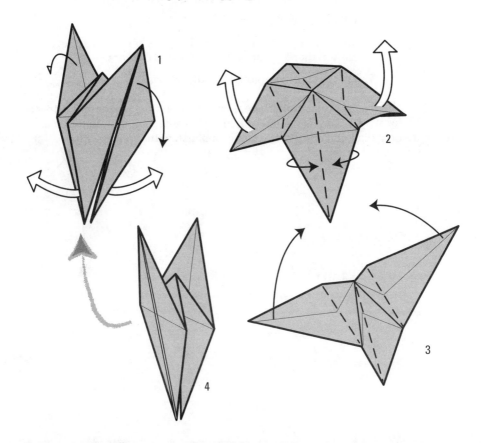

Multiform or Windmill Base

The multiform or windmill base is a versatile and logical arrangement of the paper, using 'obvious' creases. The base is called multiform because you can make several simple shapes by simply rearranging the flaps. If you arrange the flaps with rotational symmetry, the base is called a windmill base, for obvious reasons! You'll find this base in use on several traditional models, but more rarely on modern work.

1. Start with the square white side up, book-folded in half both ways and unfolded. Fold upper and lower edges to the centre.

2. Fold the left edge to the centre.

3. The drawing is enlarged. Fold the two corners to the left mid point.

4. Take hold of the original corner of the square and ease it out from behind a white layer, over to the left. (I use a pull out arrow to show where you're separating the layers.)

5. This is the result.

6. Rotate the paper and repeat the move on the matching corner, then repeat on the other two corners.

7. This is your completed multiform base.

You can mountain fold the paper in half on the horizontal centre to form a traditional catamaran. Alternatively, mountain fold in half on a diagonal to form the traditional fish with open mouth.

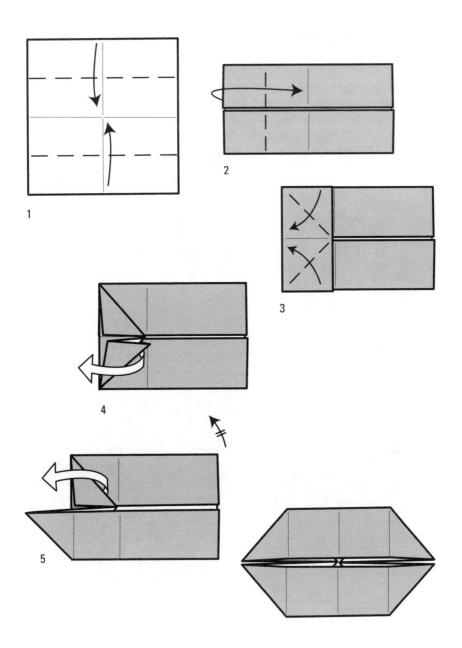

Here's how to make a windmill base.

1. Unfold your preliminary base, coloured side upwards. Fold a corner to the centre, crease, and unfold. Repeat with the three other corners.

2. Turn the paper over. Fold the lower edge to the centre, crease, and unfold. Repeat three times.

3. Refold the lower edge to the centre.

4. Fold the coloured corner down and right, as you fold the left edge to the vertical centre.

5. Rotate the paper 90 degrees and repeat the last step. Repeat on the other two sides.

6. Here's your completed windmill base.

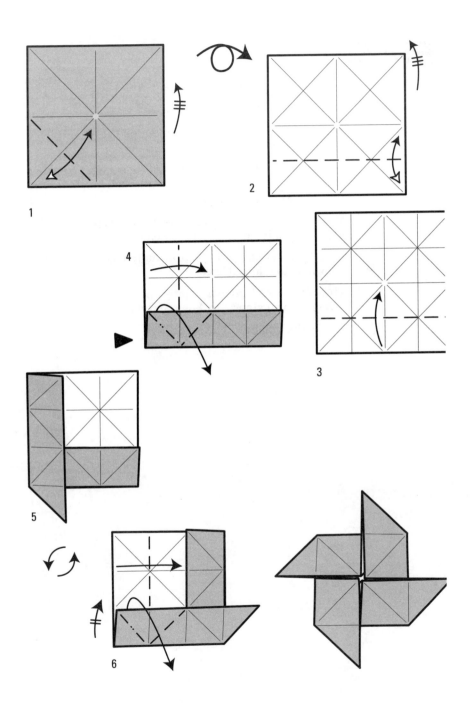

Frog Base

This is the most complex base in the book. The basic crease pattern for this base is used for the Beetle model in Chapter 7.

1. Start with a waterbomb base, colour on the outside. Fold the lower left corner to the top corner.

2. Fold the upper left edge to the vertical centre, taking two folded edges so the crease passes through four layers in total. Crease firmly and unfold.

3. Start to squash the left flap using the pre-creases. Let the lower end of the flap stay 3D to some extent.

4. Fold the lower corner to the top, flattening on the edges shown by the dotted lines.

5. This is the result, shown slightly open so you can see the layers. Repeat steps 1 to 4 on the three remaining corners.

6. This is the frog base.

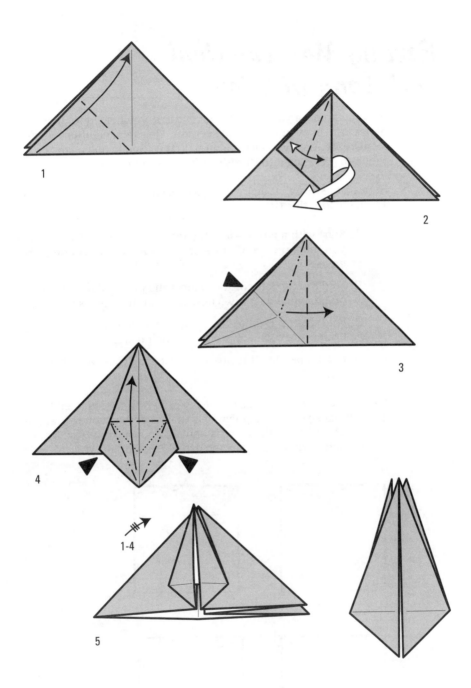

Getting Mathematical with Long Division

At some point in your origami adventures, you'll need to divide the paper into an even number of sections. Quarters, eighths, and sixteenths are easy; you just fold in half, then fold in half again as required. Dividing into thirds or fifths is slightly harder.

Here's a method that many folders use, called the *iterative* method. To divide into thirds:

1. Start with a guess – fold the top right corner over to where you think the 'third' division lies. Make a *very* gentle crease.

2. Fold the top left corner to meet the pinch. Make another pinch, equally lightly. These are your first guesses.

3. Fold the top right to the most recent pinch, make a *slightly* firmer pinch, which probably won't match the first pinch.

4. Keep repeating this process until, magically, you've established thirds.

The better your first guess is, the fewer iterations you need to make. What's actually happening is that each time you repeat the left to right process, the error is halved. Amazing but true. If you divide each third in half, you get sixths! Extraordinary!

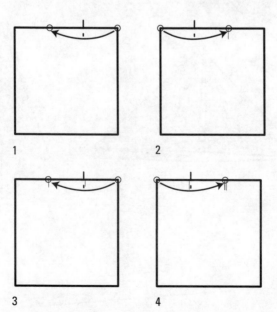

1   2

3   4

Here's an alternative method, discovered by origamist Robert Lang using his amazing reference-finder software (you give it a point, and it works out how to find that point by folding. You can download it for free from www.langorigami.com). This method is so extraordinarily simple, I'm surprised it's such a relatively recent discovery.

1. Start with a square that has a diagonal running top left to bottom right. Fold the lower edge to the diagonal, crease, and unfold.

2. Fold the right edge to the most recent crease. Then unfold.

3. Where the recent crease meets the top edge marks one third from the left!

4. In order to generate a third crease without all these location creases, fold the top left corner to the one third location.

5. This is your template.

6. Insert a fresh sheet so it meets the inside hidden edge.

7. Fold the left edge to the edge of the template, crease, and unfold.

8. Remove the template and you have a beautifully neat third crease.

The idea of using a template has a lot of merit, because it enables you to start folding without a series of creases already present and unwanted after you have your division in place.

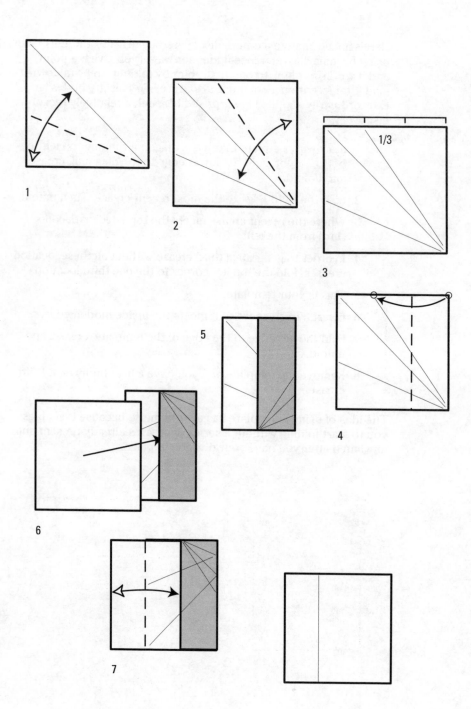

Here's a simple method of making fifths, based on a principle known as the Haga Theorem.

1. Mark the mid-point of the upper edge.

2. Mark the quarter point.

3. Fold the lower left corner to the quarter pinch.

4. Fold the upper right corner to where the coloured edge meets the white edge.

5. The right edge is now divided into one fifth and (obviously!) four fifths.

You need to locate fifths for the Four-Compartment Box in the Chapter 6, but it's a pretty uncommon starting point because it's quite tricky.

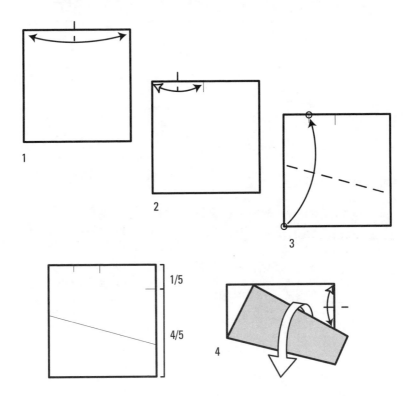

Chapter 4

Starting Simple

* *

In This Chapter

▶ Some no-fold and one-fold models

▶ Butterflies, dinosaurs, hens, and elephants

▶ Envelopes, dishes, and bookmarks

* *

*W*ho says origami has to be complicated?

Like any art or craft, origami has a complete spectrum of difficulty, ranging from so-simple-anyone-could-manage-it through to the ultra-complex-takes-several-days-to-complete designs. The temptation with any origami book is to skim through and tackle the more eye-catching projects first, only to find yourself unable to complete them due to a lack of basic skills. Confidence goes, enthusiasm goes, and before you know it, you're convinced you can't do origami and move on to brass-rubbing or hang-gliding.

So, start off at the foot of the paper ladder and see how simple origami can be.

If you struggle with a specific model, lay it to one side and come back to it later. The problem may disappear overnight or it may last a little while longer! I recommend that you start with a large sheet of paper (at least 20 centimetres by 20 centimetres) for anything with more than eight or so steps. Also, fold each model several times, to make sure you thoroughly understand how it works.

Black Sheep Down a Mine

This design is by Bronco Sinkin. The mine depicted must be completely dark – any miner's head-lamps would spoil the effect.

1. Start with a square, black side upwards.
2. The model is complete.

You'll spot certain similarities between this and the following well-known design.

A Sheep During Winter

Ron 'Bonsai' Nichols came up with this one.

1. Start with a square, white side upwards.
2. The model is complete.

Some people find the sheep itself hard to spot – it's in the top right corner, of course.

The Horizon

Allow me to introduce the genre called *one-crease folding*, for reasons I've never discovered. This creation is by Boris Chanson-Lion.

1. Start with a square white side upwards. Fold up part of the bottom half.

2. The model is complete.

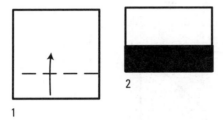

The possibilities with one crease are literally infinite, because you can make the crease wherever you want. The following design is a variation.

Slightly Seasick

Here's another gem from Boris Chanson-Lion.

1. Start with a square white side upwards. Fold up part of the bottom half at a slight angle.

2. The model is complete.

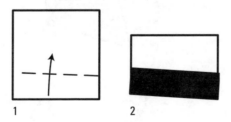

I'm hoping that you're already realising that origami is the hobby for you.

Sailboat

It's time to accelerate onwards and upwards with yet another crease!

1. Start with a square white side upwards. Fold a diagonal from bottom left to top right.

2. Fold the lower corner upwards at a slight angle.

3. This is the result. Turn the paper over.

4. Your sailboat is complete.

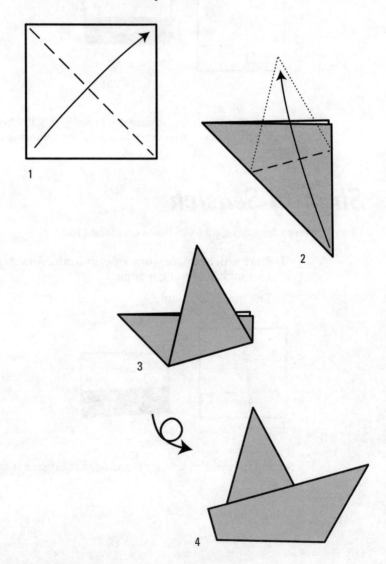

Flower

Adding yet another crease means the design becomes more sophisticated.

1. Start with a square white side upwards, corner towards you. Fold in half from bottom to top along the diagonal.

2. Fold the left half of the lower edge upwards to somewhere just to the left of the top corner.

3. Repeat the fold on the right-hand side.

4. Your flower is complete. I hope you're feeling that you have a future in origami. Hang on to this thought; it'll help later on.

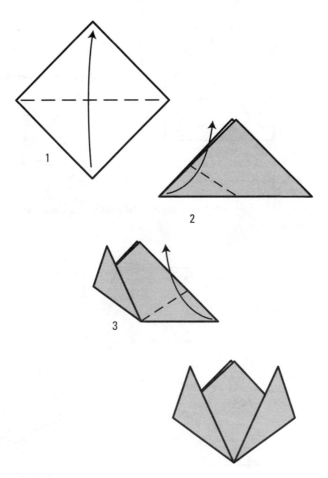

T-Rex Head

Feeling brave? It's time to progress to a four-crease design of mine.

1. Start with a square white side upwards. Fold a diagonal from top left to bottom right.

2. Fold the right-hand vertical edge to the left and slightly down.

3. Fold the lower flap upwards and to the left.

4. The model should look something like this, but that depends on exactly how you made the last two steps. Fold the first layer of the small triangular flap over.

5. Roar!

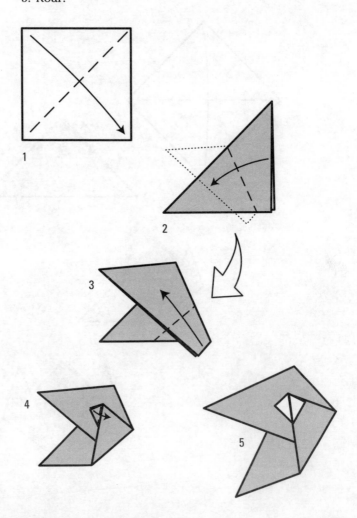

Bookmark

This model of mine is typical of the type of design you can create yourself with a bit of experimentation. Having a simple target shape helps the challenge, because you can focus on an elegant method and not worry about complex geometry.

1. Start with a square, white side upwards. Fold in half from bottom to top along a diagonal, then unfold.
2. Fold from side to side, but only crease the lower half of the paper. Unfold.
3. Fold the upper corner to the centre of the paper.
4. Rotate the paper 180 degrees and repeat step 3.
5. Fold in half from bottom to top.
6. Fold the left-hand side to lie on the vertical centre crease.
7. Repeat on the right.
8. This is the result. Turn the paper over.
9. Fold the upper flaps in half downwards, crease, and unfold.
10. Fold the flaps down again, this time tucking them into the pocket.
11. Rotate the paper to this position for the finished bookmark.

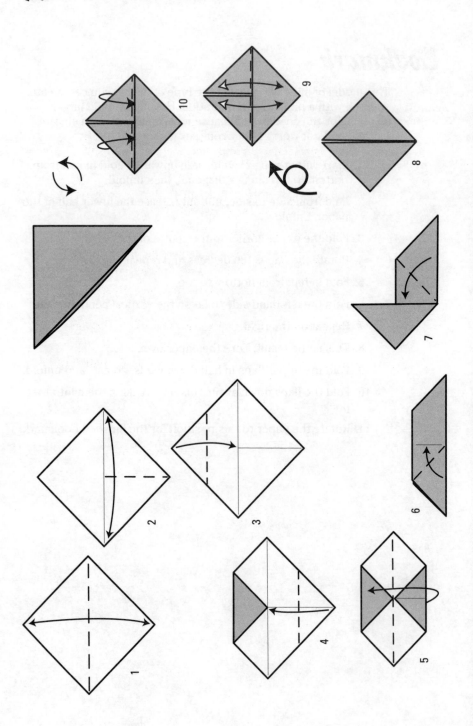

3D Star

Rachel Katz is a fine teacher of origami and so knows exactly what a model needs to make it easy for beginners. This design takes five identical folded units (or *modules*) and slots them into each other to form a surprising 3D star. With any designs that interlock, you need to take special care to fold accurately, or the resulting model may not hold together well.

1. Coloured side up, fold one side to the opposite side both ways and unfold. Turn the paper over.

2. Crease both diagonals.

3. Use the creases shown to collapse the paper into the waterbomb base (Chapter 3 describes bases).

4. Fold both outer corners to the top corner, crease, and unfold. Repeat behind.

5. This is the basic unit. Make another four in the same way.

6. Arrange two units as shown and slide the right-hand one into the left-hand one. Each flap goes into a matching pocket.

7. When the units are firmly interlocked, open out the pocket at the top, squashing the pocket in half, and then let it open again.

8. Add the third unit in the same way and continue with the remaining two units.

9. Your star is complete.

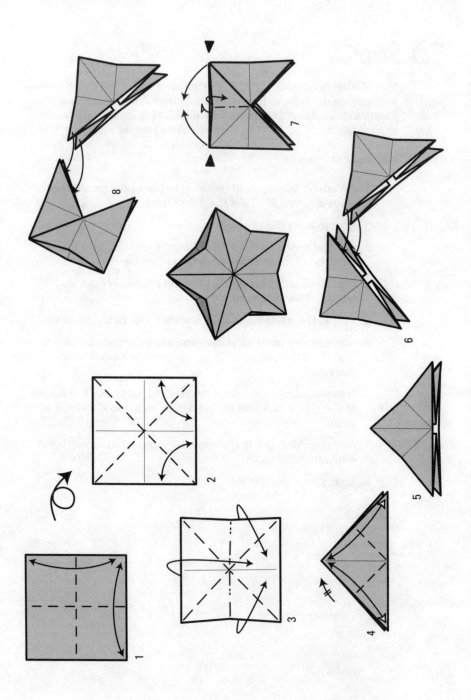

Coin Trick

Here's a simple fold that you can use to boost your income. You
fold a triangular shape with 2 pockets, open one slightly and slip a
coin inside. With an elaborate flourish, you make the coin vanish!

The model needs a 2 by 1 rectangle, which you can easily make by
folding a square in half, as shown in step 1. However, this is, in fact, a
little wasteful, because every fold is duplicated through both layers.

So, to the horrified faces of paper-folders worldwide, I'll reveal
another way to create the required rectangle: cut it in half! The cutting symbol is easily recognisable. (Actually, cutting isn't as heretical
as you might think – many older, traditional origami designs incorpo-
rate cuts and if you need a triangle, special rectangle, pentagon, or
hexagon to fold with, you generally have to cut paper to produce it.)

Most modern creators wouldn't dream of using cuts to form the
actual model. The beauty of origami is to use only folding techniques to solve the design challenge – simply cutting out the shape
of a given subject is far less impressive and satisfying.

1. Start with your cut rectangle, white side upwards, fold in
   half from left to right.
2. Fold in half from bottom to top, crease, and unfold.
3. Fold the lower left corner to the diagonally opposite halfway point.
4. Rotate the paper 180 degrees and repeat the last fold.
5. Fold the lower corner to the nearest right hand corner.
6. Rotate the paper 180 degrees. Fold the lower corner in the
   same way, but unfold it after creasing.
7. Fold the upper triangular flap down (using the crease you
   made in step 2).
8. Tuck the lower flap all the way into the pocket of the section you just swung down.
9. The trick is ready for use.

The routine

1. Hold the model with one pocket open at the top and the
   other towards your hand. Place a coin inside.
2. Move your hand around to distract the viewer, rotate
   the model by 90 degrees, and turn it over so it appears
   unchanged, but the pocket with the coin is towards your
   hand.
3. Open the 'new' pocket to show that the coin has vanished.

If you're particularly adept, you can let the coin slip into your palm, and unfold the model to show that the coin's vanished.

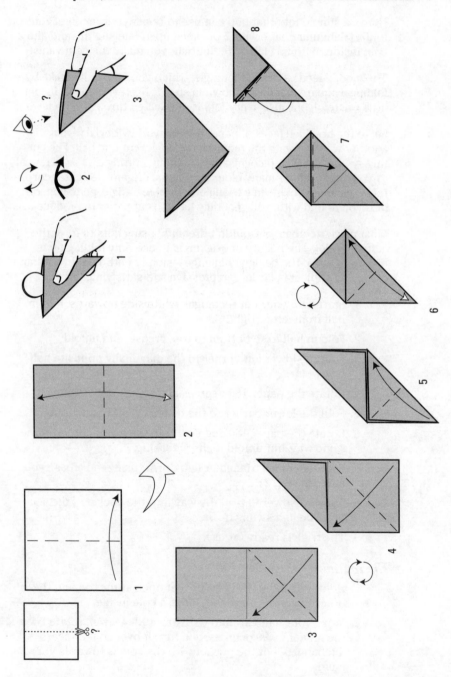

Japanese Schoolgirl

Despite the fact that almost every human face is both complex and unique, you can use origami as a means of reducing faces to their basic constituents, almost like a cartoon face. Although you use only a few simple creases, everyone can still recognise the subject. This design of mine is almost entirely valley or mountain creases, except for the final stages, where you use a squash fold to shape the hair and cheeks of the face in one move (refer to Chapter 1 which explains the squash fold).

1. Start with a square, white side upwards, with a corner towards you. Crease and unfold both diagonals.

2. Fold the lower corner to the centre.

3. Fold the lower section in half again.

4. Fold the same section upwards using the original diagonal crease.

5. Fold the coloured section over, crease, and unfold.

6. Starting just left of the centre, fold the left corner upwards to match the dotted line.

7. Repeat on the right side.

8. This is the result.

9. Turn the paper over. Fold the lower tip upwards to form the chin.

10. Fold the lower left raw edge, making a crease between the corner of the small white triangle and the end of the existing horizontal crease. Squash the paper with a new mountain crease, flattening underneath on the existing crease.

11. Repeat the move on the right side.

12. This is the result.

13. Turn the paper over for the finished design.

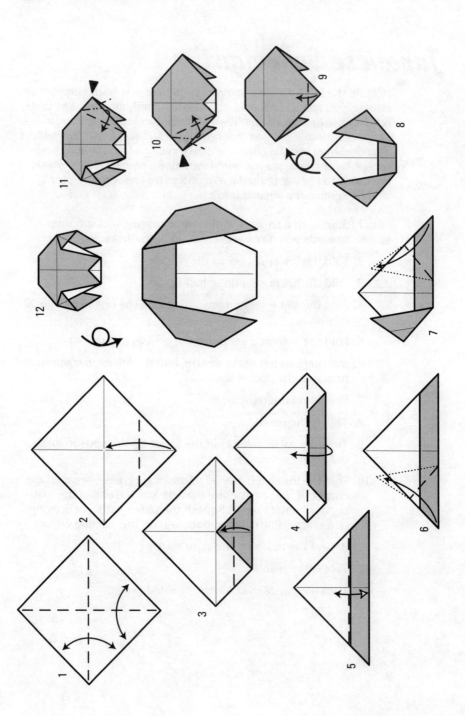

Three Crease Head

Paul Jackson's design has only three creases, so it's hard to go far wrong. This fold is an example of minimal origami, named for obvious reasons. The idea is to capture the essence of the subject as simply as possible and not worry about the fine details like how many legs a spider has or how many fingers a hand has.

Here you simply have a nose, an eyeline, and a hairline. (Clearly the latter is a bonus feature, as many older men don't have a hairline.) Another exciting aspect of this model is that each fold rarely has a precise location, so you can create a variety of interpretations and express your creativity! Sometimes a small change can produce a big result, so make lots of models, seeing whether changing a certain angle gives better, or worse results.

1. Start with a square, coloured side upwards. Fold about one third over from the right (Chapter 3 explains how to find one third).

2. Fold the coloured flap behind at a slight angle – check the next drawing for guidance. The white corner that sticks out becomes the nose, so use that to help judge the angle.

3. Fold the upper section down at a slight angle, adjust to suit your own taste, then flatten.

4. The completed head.

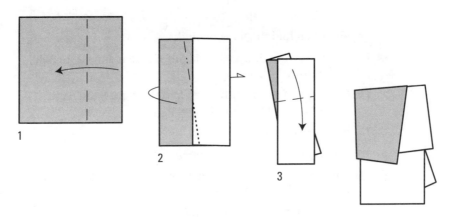

Dunce's Cap

Here's a design of mine inspired by my friend Rachel Katz, with an origami 'D' to go with the dunce's cap. You're not supposed to use glue in origami, so you need to rub both the cap and the D onto your hair to create sufficient static electricity to hold them together – or a stapler might be more effective!

1. Start with a square, white side upwards, with a corner towards you. Fold the right-hand corner to the lower corner, making an incomplete crease as shown. This crease is only used to create the required angle, so make it as gently as you can.

2. Starting the crease at the top corner, fold the left corner to meet the crease you made in step 1. Using these two reference points, there's only one correct placement for this crease and it generates an angle of 60 degrees – isn't that magical?

3. Unfold the paper.

4. Fold in half from bottom to top.

5. Make a fold as in step 2, using the top corner as one reference and the lower end of the crease as the other.

6. Refold the left side over to the right.

7. This is the result. Turn the paper over.

8. Fold the lower flaps upwards.

9. Mountain fold the flaps behind.

10. Pull the layers down, allowing the hidden ends to remain folded over.

11. Open the paper slightly, then fold the right-hand flap upwards, tucking it into the pocket.

12. Repeat on the left-hand side.

13. Press the sides slightly to open the cap.

14. For the 'D', start with a small square and fold the edges in following the order shown.

15. Fold the white corners behind.

16. Add the D to the cap by fair means or foul.

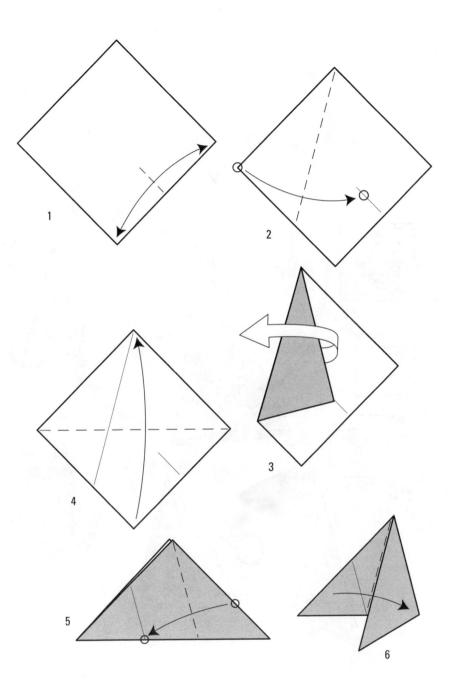

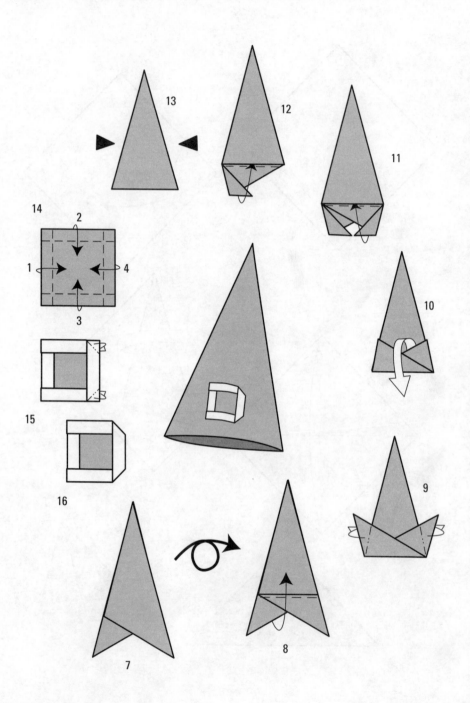

Miniphant

Although simple, the miniphant by Mike Dilkes is quite sophisticated visually. It's also a wonderful way to practise your reverse
folding technique!

1. Start with a square, white side upwards. Fold in half along a
   diagonal.

2. Fold the upper corner down to match the dotted line,
   crease, and unfold. Note roughly where the crease starts on
   the left.

3. Make another pre-crease on the left.

4. Inside reverse the point on the left.

5. The dotted line shows an x-ray view of where the paper
   lies. Inside reverse the top point. Be careful to use the
   existing crease and not to add any new ones!

6. Fold the outer edges of the trunk to meet the inner edges.

7. Fold in paper to shape the front of the elephant. You may
   need to hold the paper in the air to do this.

8. Here's a miniphant on parade.

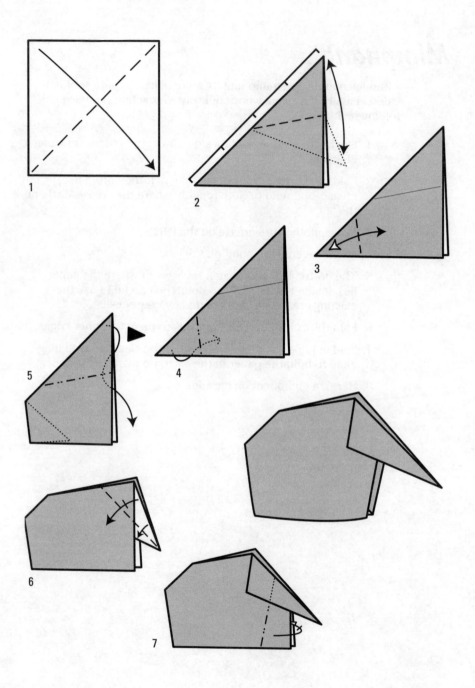

Elephant's Head

Here's an example of how one design can be quickly adapted to create another. When I was playing around with the folding sequence for the Dunce's Cap, I spotted something that looked like an elephant's head (paper-folders are good at this type of thing).

Look closely at step 8 – you form an inside reverse fold on the right, while leaving the left side unfolded. This requires a certain delicacy of touch, which I'm sure you all possess more or less.

1. Start with a square, white side upwards, with a corner towards you. Fold the right-hand corner to the lower corner, making an incomplete crease as in the previous model.

2. Starting the crease at the top corner, fold the left corner to meet the crease you made in step 1.

3. Fold the right-hand side over to the left.

4. Fold the top corner to the bottom

5. This is where I spotted a potential elephant! Unfold back to the square.

6. Add a crease that starts at the intersection of creases and extends out to the raw edge. As you make the fold, you can easily see reference creases.

7. Repeat the last step on the other side.

8. Fold the top down, using the two existing valley creases. The mountain crease is formed in the right place as you flatten the paper.

9. This is the result. Open and repeat step 8 on the left-hand side, as indicated by the 'repeat' arrow.

10. Now make the move on both sides, overlapping the layers inside (it doesn't matter which layer is on which).

11. This is the result. You can stop here if you're happy! Otherwise, turn the paper over.

12. Make a shaping crease on both ears to fit your own vision of an elephant.

13. Fold the lower corner up as far as it'll go.

14. Turn the paper over for the completed profile. You can stop here if you want, or . . .

15. If you're feeling ambitious, add these gentle 3D shaping creases to give the model some depth.

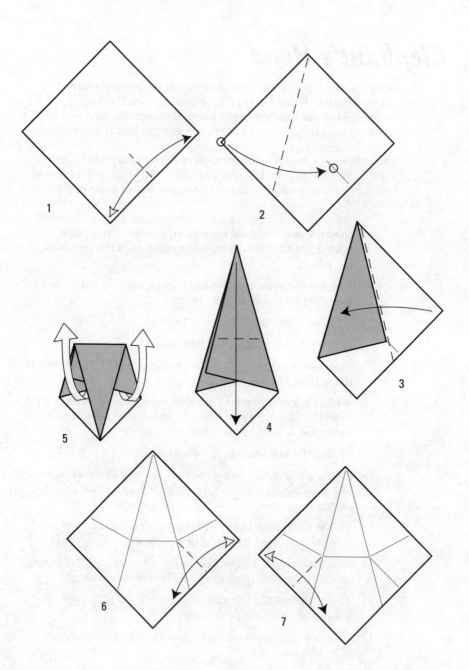

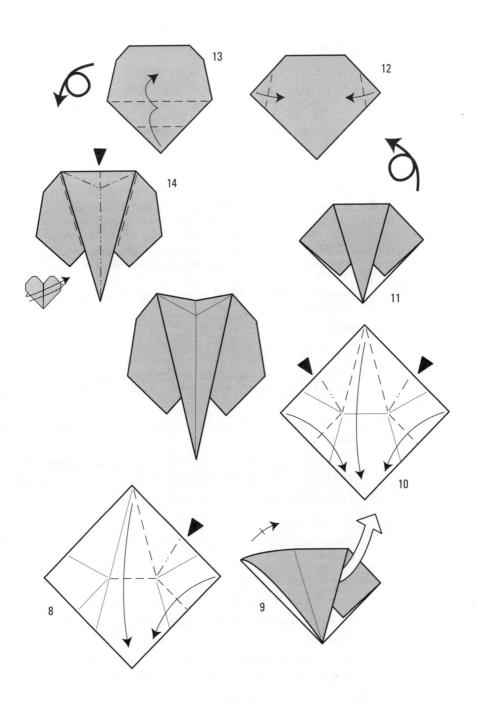

Shell

Stephen Casey is a relatively unknown Australian origami expert who's been producing excellent origami models for well over twenty years. Don't let the number of steps deter you – although I could have combined some of the steps to produce fewer diagrams, focusing on just one step at a time is always easier. Just take each fold as it comes and concentrate on folding neatly.

You can try folding this design in the imaginary world – read the diagrams, take an imaginary sheet of paper, and work your way through the sequence a couple of times. Then use real paper and see if you find the steps easier to follow. Many a time I've reluctantly tackled a set of diagrams, only to discover a wonderful move, or a finished result that the diagrams don't do justice to.

1. Start with a square, white side upwards. Crease both diagonals.

2. Fold in half from top to bottom.

3. Fold in half from left to right.

4. Rotate the paper slightly so the original corners are towards you. Fold the lower corner to the top, crease, and unfold.

5. Fold the lower corner to the most recent crease, then unfold.

6. At risk of repeating myself, fold the lower corner to the most recent crease, then unfold.

7. Fold over on the horizontal diagonal.

8. Fold the lower corner to the centre.

9. Swing the same double layer over on the horizontal diagonal.

10. Fold the lower corner to the centre.

11. Take the lower horizontal folded edge to the centre.

12. Swing the same double layer over on the horizontal diagonal.

13. You've added the horizontal stripes; now you need to shape the paper into 3D. Turn the paper over.

14. Fold in half from bottom to top.

15. Fold both sides to meet the vertical centre.

16. This is the result. Turn the paper over.

17. Fold the small triangular flaps over, crease well, and unfold.

18. Open the pocket slightly and tuck the same flaps inside the model.

19. Open and squash the paper slightly to make it 3D.

20. Here's your completed shell.

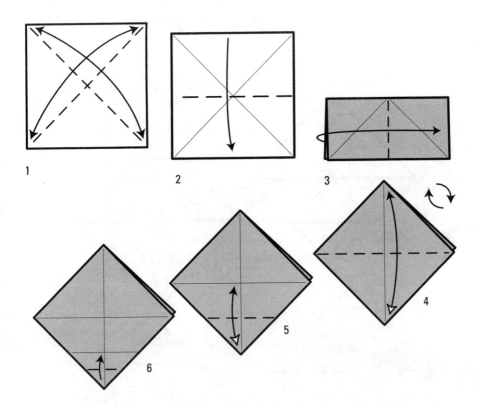

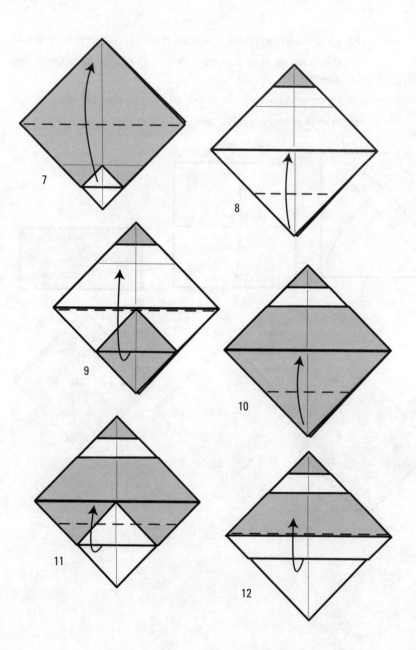

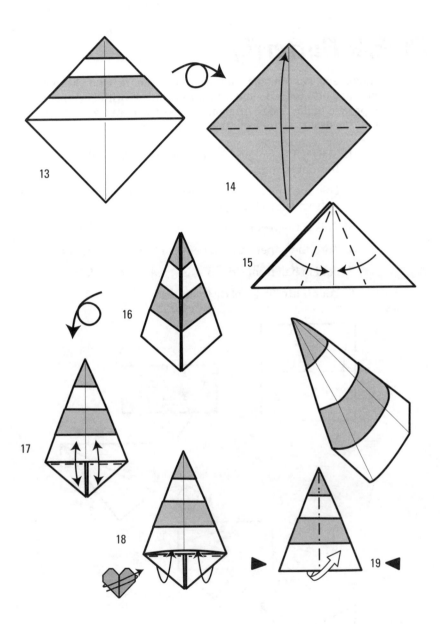

Thoki's Butterfly

Thoki Yenn was a magical folder from Denmark, who alternately charmed and baffled almost everyone he met with his unusual approach to life and to origami. He was fascinated with geometry and this design arose from that fascination.

1. Start with a square, white side upwards. Fold in half from bottom to top.

2. Fold the top left corner down, making the crease run from bottom left to top right.

3. This is the result.

4. Turn the paper over. Repeat the last step on this side.

5. Fold in half from side to side, crease, and unfold.

6. Your butterfly is ready to flutter.

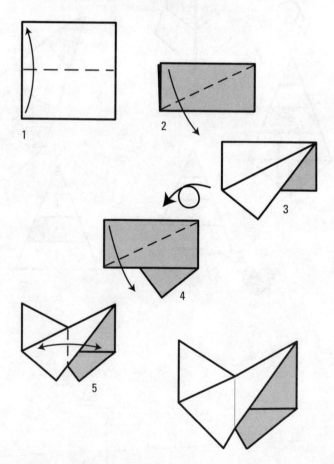

Boaz's Butterfly

Origamist Boaz Shuval uses geometry too, but divides the paper into *thirds* before applying the same technique as Thoki's Butterfly, resulting in a related but more sophisticated model, which he arrived at independently from Thoki.

1. Start with a square, white side upwards. Divide into thirds horizontally, using the method I outline in Chapter 3. Leave the right side folded in.

2. Fold the flap out, making a crease that runs from bottom right to top left of the upper flap.

3. This is the result.

4. Fold the left-hand side across.

5. Repeat step three, folding in the opposite direction.

6. This is the result. Turn the paper over.

7. Make yet another identical crease through the upper layer.

8. Fold the model in half.

9. Leaving a small gap (which forms the body), fold the upper wing back down.

10. Fold the upper wing down to match the lower one.

11. Open the model out, leaving some degree of 3Dness in it.

12. The butterfly is complete.

Have a go at folding the next logical version of the butterfly, by dividing the paper into quarters and folding using a similar method as this.

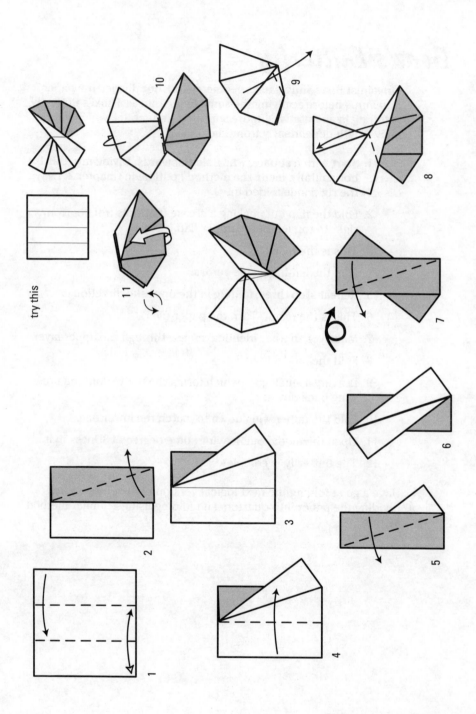

Triplane

Time for some fun! Everyone loves a paper aeroplane and you probably know at least one design. Many of the classics go back a long time, but designers now apply modern origami techniques in search of the two main competitive categories: flying longer distances and staying in the air for a longer time. As with the Dunce's Cap and Elephant Head (earlier on in this chapter), you have a simple and accurate method for creating the required angle. The trisecting of the angle led to the name of my design – apologies if you hoped it would have three wings!

People often make paper planes, launch them, and reject the design if it doesn't fly well. You can make three simple adjustments to launching a plane, each of which affects the flight characteristics. These are the speed of launch, the angle of launch, and the angle of the wings to the body. Every design has a perfect combination of these three elements so try adjusting them one at a time to see what effect it has on the flight. In other words, if the plane doesn't fly properly first time, adjust, and keep adjusting! After a while, you'll be able to get this model right fairly quickly.

1. Start with a square, white side upwards. Crease in half from side to side, then open.

2. Fold left and right sides to meet in the centre.

3. This is an enlarged view. Fold the sides to the centre, creasing (approximately) the top third only.

4. Turn the paper over. Starting the crease in the centre of the top edge, fold the left corner to lie somewhere on the right-hand quarter crease. Check the next diagram for guidance.

5. This is what you're aiming for. Crease well and unfold. Make sure you understand the diagram before moving on.

6. Repeat the move on the right-hand side.

7. You've outlined two sides of an equilateral triangle. Open the two flaps from underneath.

8. Turn the paper over. Fold the upper side down, making sure the crease passes through the base of the triangular creases.

9. Use these creases to make a squash fold – it's easier than it looks!

10. Repeat on the other side, tucking the point inside the pocket on the right.

11. Fold the narrow flap upwards as far as you can, without tearing the paper.

12. Mountain fold the plane in half.

13. Take the first folded edge on the left across to meet the vertical folded edge on the right.

14. Repeat the move on the underside.

15. Open the wings so they're at a slight upwards angle. Your Triplane is ready for take-off!

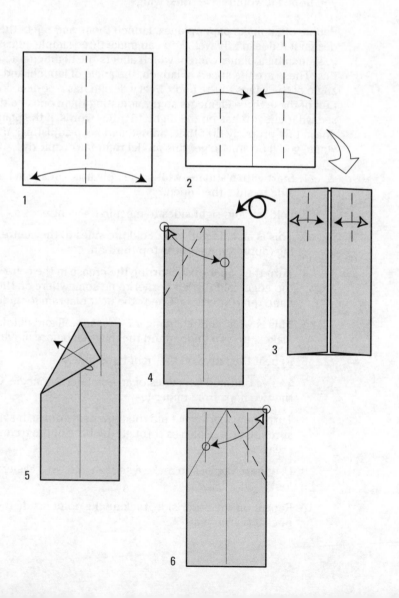

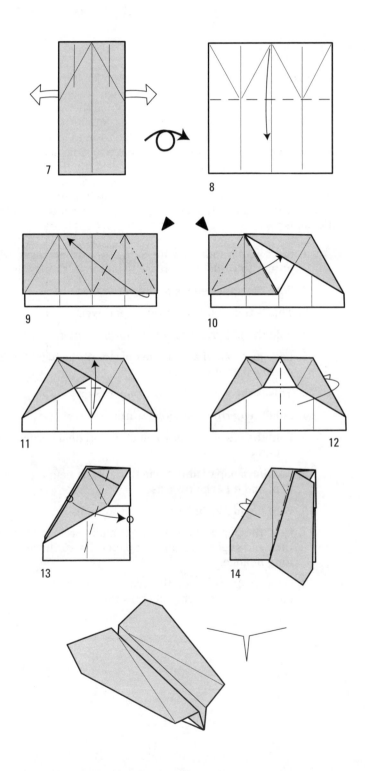

Chick

Kunihiko Kasahara is one of the Japanese Masters of origami, who has created many beautiful, simple designs over the last 40 years and written over 1,000 origami books along the way. This classic model dates from the mid 1960s. It's essentially a series of reverse folds, but the method used here enables you to form the reverses without even realising it. When you have to make a reverse fold, see if you can open the paper, make a pleat, then close the paper again (not always possible). Step 11 is an interesting move, where you pull apart two layers of paper , then flatten the paper into a new position. You do this technique in the air, rather than flat on the table.

1. Start with a square, white side upwards, arranged with the corner towards you. Crease in half from side to side.

2. Fold the upper edges to the vertical centre.

3. This is the result. Turn the paper over.

4. Fold the upper corner to the lower corner.

5. Leaving a gap of about one quarter of the height, fold the narrow flap upwards.

6. This is the result. Turn the paper over.

7. Fold the narrow flap downwards.

8. Fold the lower corner to meet the original corners of the square.

9. Leaving a gap of about one third of the height of the small flap, fold it back upwards.

10. Fold the model in half from left to right.

11. Hold the paper where the right-hand circle is, then rotate the head slightly, easing out paper. Check the next drawing for guidance.

12. Do a similar move on the head, easing the beak down and flattening the paper so it stays there.

13. Your chick is complete.

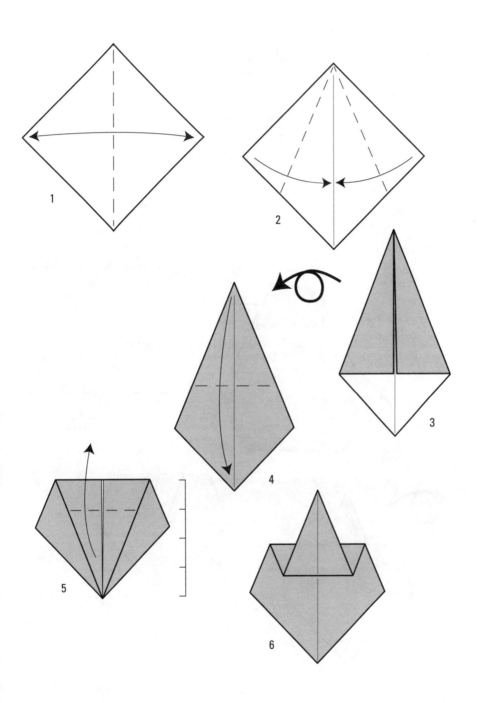

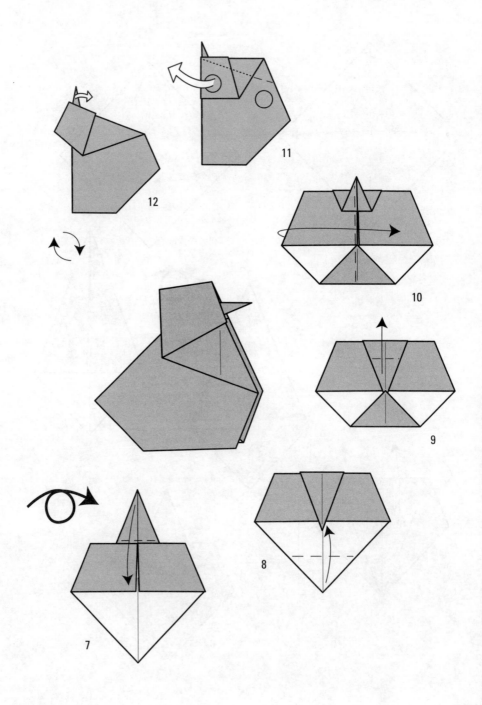

Fishy Sequence

Here's a simple fish design of mine that transforms into an alien with a narrow head, an alien with a square head, and finally a butterfly. Some imagination is required to see the subject, but if you didn't have imagination, origami probably wouldn't appeal to you!

In this model, the fold at step 2 determines the shape of the fish. Can you see any other possibilities lying within the paper?

1. Start with a square, white side upwards, arranged with the corner towards you. Crease in half from top to bottom.

2. Fold the right corner to slightly past the approximate centre of the paper.

3. This is the result. Turn the paper over.

4. Starting the creases at the right-hand corners, fold the lower and upper corners to lie on the centre crease.

5. Here's the fish.

6. Fold the tip of the left-hand corner over. Rotate the paper 90 degrees clockwise.

7. Here's the first Alien Head.

8. Mountain fold the top of the head behind. Unfold the lower flap from underneath.

9. Fold over the tip of the lower corner.

10. Rotate the paper 180 degrees for the second Alien Head.

11. Refold the top of the head behind.

12. Turn the paper over for the butterfly.

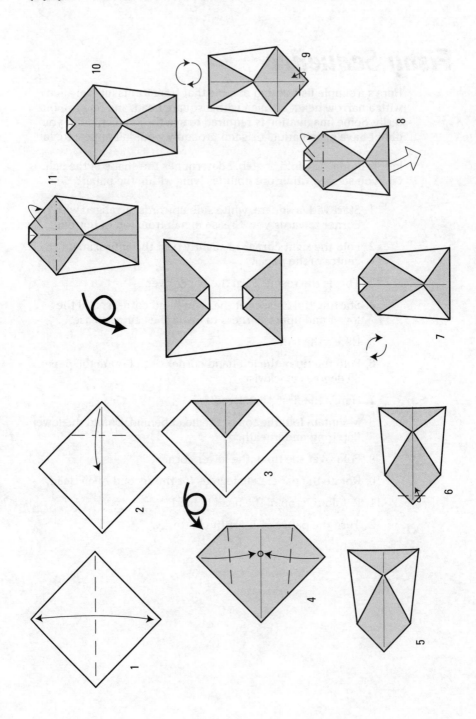

Fish

This model is an altogether different approach to an origami fish. In fact, one of the chief joys in origami is comparing how two (or more) different creators tackle the same subject in their own style. Stephen Casey is from Australia, so naturally has an inverted perspective on life and his own unique approach to folding – he apparently created this design at night, while singing. It was salmon chanted evening, I cod you not.

The design uses a 2 by 1 rectangle, otherwise known as half a square.

1. Start with half a square, white side upwards. Fold in half from short edge to short edge.

2. Fold the bottom right corner to the top left, crease, and unfold.

3. Fold over the first edge at the top to lie on the crease you made in step 2.

4. Fold the white section in half.

5. Fold over the short coloured edge to lie against the white flap.

6. Swing over the flap on a crease running from bottom right to the left-hand corner.

7. Now fold over the same flap again so that the back of the tail is vertical.

8. This is the result. Turn the paper over from top to bottom (the rotated turn-over symbol indicates this).

9. Fold in half from top left to bottom right, crease, and unfold.

10. Repeat steps 3 to 7 on this side.

11. Fold the lower corner over, tucking it under the white flap.

12. Turn the paper over. Repeat the previous step.

13. The fish is 'fin'ished.

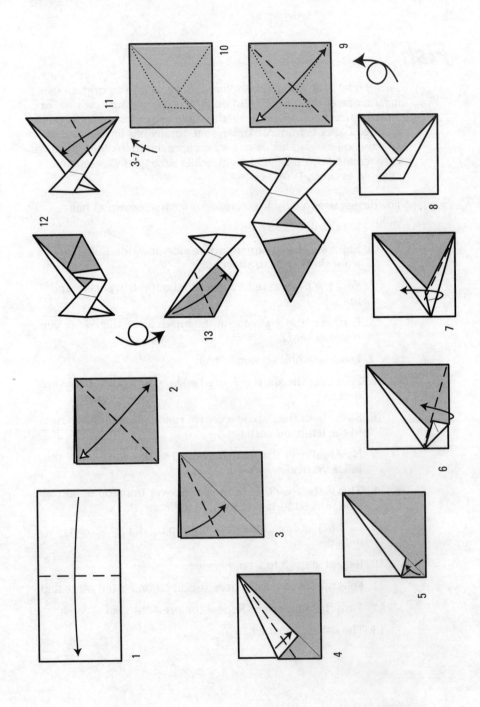

Biscuit Packet Closure

You deserve a bit of a break, having folded lots of designs. So brew up a nice cup of tea, grab a packet of biscuits, and eat a few. As any confirmed biscuit fan knows, you want your treasures in prime condition. What generally happens is that you put the packet away and the contents go soft. Here's an exciting design by Edwin Corrie to keep your biccies fresh!

1. Carefully open a packet of biscuits and eat at least half the contents. Press two opposite sides together.

2. Fold the flap over to one side.

3. Fold the sides in to meet in the centre.

4. Make two valley folds and tuck the flap under the layers. If the narrow flap is too short, eat a few more biscuits.

5. Complete.

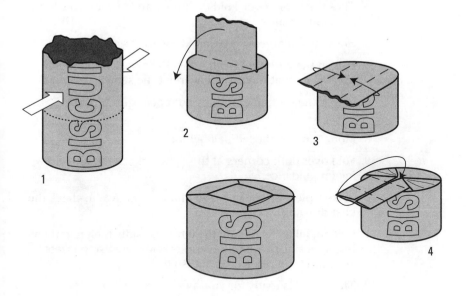

A Fishy Tale

Michel Grand is a Frenchman with a great sense of humour. As well as designing numerous envelopes, he also enjoys puzzles and jokes. This model is an example of *storigami*, where the folding (or unfolding) of a model is accompanied by a story of some kind. In the early 20th century, many magicians used origami in their acts, often incorporating tales to help the performance flow.

The design only works as part of a story. If you look at the individual stages, they appear incomplete and inconclusive, but within the context of a story, they make perfect sense.

1. Start with a square, white side upwards, with a corner towards you. Crease and unfold both diagonals.
2. Fold the top and bottom corners to the centre.
3. Fold the inner corners out to the edges.
4. Turn the paper over. Fold the upper and lower edges to the horizontal centre.
5. Here's an enlarged view. Unfold the top two layers.
6. Fold in the corners shown – check the next step for guidance. Note that the two folds aren't the same!
7. Refold the section upwards and repeat the steps on the lower half.
8. Mountain fold the left half behind.
9. Fold over both corners at the right – check the next drawing for guidance.
10. Make a pleat on the upper left-hand layer. Again, check the next drawing.
11. Pull out all the layers on the left-hand side, then fold them back, tucking the exposed corners into the two pockets shown. This looks tricky, but isn't!
12. The model is ready for your performance. Rotate 90 degrees anti-clockwise.

The performance

13. Here's a heart – it means someone loves something. What could it be?
14. (Turn over top to bottom.) A fish! Who loves fish?
15. (Pull layer out of corners underneath and unfold upwards.) A cat!

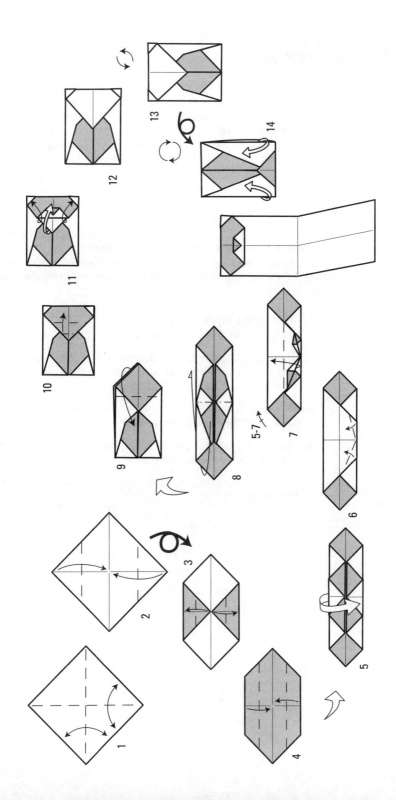

Fox's Head

This design only has a few creases, but it requires some care and concentration because it's three-dimensional and incorporates curved folds. You can make the model several times to get a good feel for it and to make the final result symmetrical. You can use the 'wet-folding' technique for designs like this. Fold with thickish paper, such as Canson, Elephant Hide, or Wyndstone (all described in Chapter 1), and lightly dampen the paper before folding. When the paper dries out, it's fixed in the final shape and so is much more robust.

The crease in step 2 actually consists of two straight creases that are joined with a curved fold – you'll see how this works when you make it. Excluding step 4, the design is by Wayne Brown. I suggested the extra step and Wayne felt it deserved compositional credit.

1. Start with a square, white side upwards, with a corner towards you. Fold the lower corner to the top.

2. Holding the paper in the air, carefully put in a slightly curved crease where shown, pressing the paper into 3D. Try to make it symmetrical.

3. This step is seen from the viewpoint of the eye. Fold the flaps on either side upwards.

4. This step is seen from the viewpoint of the eye. Fold the back of the 'ear flaps' behind with a sharp mountain fold on either side.

5. Complete!

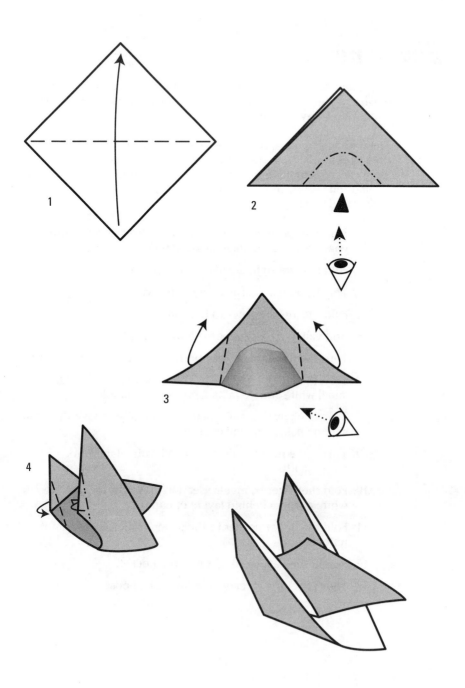

Envelope

Doris Lauinger is a talented creator who lives near Bonn in Germany. She came up with this clever envelope design and my good friend Wayne Brown modified it a little.

The folding sequence has quite a few 'turn over' symbols but they're essential to make all the pre-creases correctly. The point of a pre-crease is to have the crease ready prepared with the proper orientation (valley or mountain) by the time you need it during the assembly sequence.

1. Start with a square, white side up, with a corner towards you. Crease both diagonals and unfold.

2. Fold left and right corners to the centre.

3. This is the result. Turn the paper over.

4. Fold the lower corner to the centre.

5. Add valley creases along the white edges.

6. Turn the paper over. Fold both lower corners to the centre.

7. Turn the paper over again. Are you dizzy yet? Fold the small white square in half, crease, and unfold.

8. Turn back over again. Open and carefully squash the white section using existing creases.

9. This is the result. Pull out a small white flap from underneath.

10. Fold the lower triangular section upwards, tucking the white corners behind layers of paper.

11. Fold the upper corner to the lower corner, crease, and unfold.

12. Refold the flap, tucking it into the pocket.

13. Your envelope is ready to address and post.

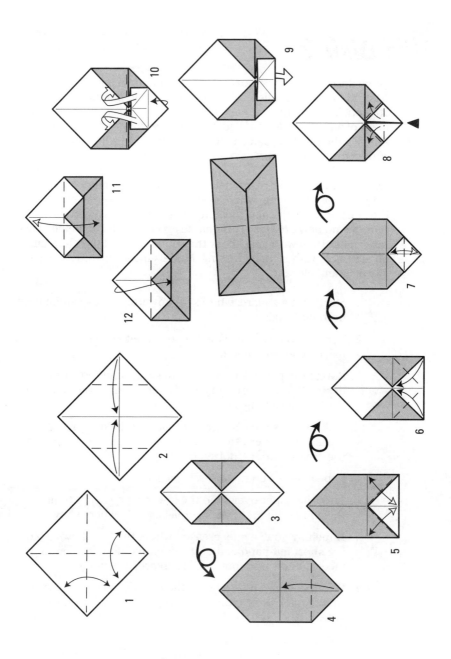

Ali's Dish 2

I love designing dishes, boxes, and containers of any kind. The basic concept is simple – fold the sides up and persuade them to stay up, 'locking' the paper so it stays in 3D. This dish is a development of an earlier design, dedicated to my (long-suffering) wife Alison, who has long since reconciled herself to a life of poverty, supporting an origamist.

As with other geometric models in this book, this model uses extensive pre-creasing, where every crease you need is put in at the start of the sequence, meaning that the final assembly stage requires no new creases. This enables you to focus on being accurate rather than worrying about the sequence, and then to focus on assembly rather than creasing. Models made this way are generally neat and elegant.

1. Start with a square, white side upwards. Crease and unfold both diagonals.

2. Turn the paper over. Fold the lower left edge to the diagonal, crease, and unfold.

3. Rotate the paper 90 degrees clockwise, and repeat the folds in step 2 (don't turn the paper over again!). Continue with the two remaining sides.

4. Make a crease that's a mirror image of the one in step 2, but crease only where shown, as far as you can. Don't extend the crease into the dotted line.

5. Repeat step 4 on the other three sides.

6. Turn the paper over. Fold the lower right corner to meet the end of the first crease, creasing only where shown.

7. Hopefully you've only creased where the bar shows! Fold the short left-hand end of the coloured double layer up to meet the raw horizontal edge, crease, and unfold.

8. Fold the same short edge to the crease you've just made. Unfold back to the square and repeat steps 6–8 on each side.

9. Folding edges away from you, put in the creases shown to form the first corner of the paper into 3D. This is the underside of the dish.

10. Fold the corner over using a crease – thanks to the pre-creasing, the crease is already in place for you.

11. Tuck the end of the flap into the pocket underneath it and give the paper a good squeeze to firm up the corner. Repeat steps 9–11 on each corner.

12. Turn over for the finished dish – gently press from underneath to slightly raise the centre, but keep the creases intact. Fill with paper frogs and sweeties!

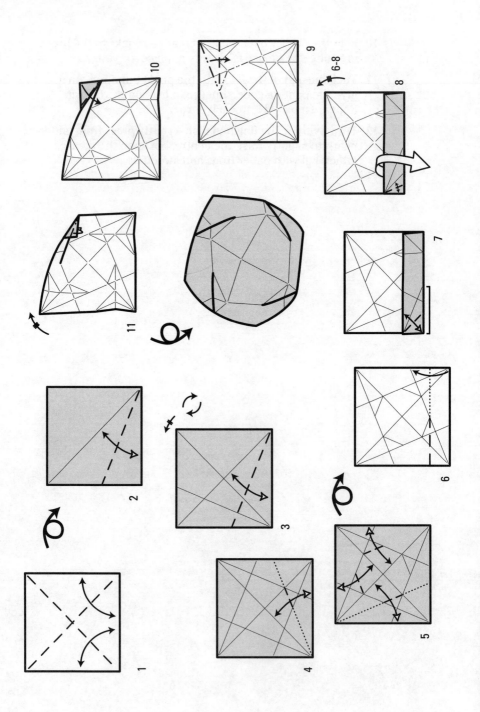

Pureland Figure

Marc Kirschenbaum is an American who, unlike many creators, seems equally at home creating simple models as he does ultra-complex ones. Here's a design he created in response to a challenge set to create a human figure using only valley and mountain folds (no reverse folds, sinks, or complicated manoeuvres like that). This technique, known as *pureland* was proposed by John Smith from England, who felt it would result in simpler models, more suitable for teaching young or novice folders.

While assisting the novice folder, the pureland technique actually presents a challenge for the designer, because he or she must avoid using standard techniques to shape the subject, using their ingenuity and vision instead.

1. Start with a square, coloured side upwards. Crease in half from side to side.

2. Fold each half of the lower edge to lie on the vertical centre crease.

3. Turn the paper over. Fold both lower white edges to the vertical centre, allowing flaps to pop out from underneath (otherwise known as 'flipping your flaps').

4. Fold the upper edge down to meet the top corner of the white square shape.

5. This is the result. Turn the paper over.

6. Fold each half of the upper edge down to lie on the vertical centre.

7. Turn the paper over. Fold the lower section upwards as far as it will go.

8. Clever isn't it? Fold the single layers over towards the centre and turn the paper over.

9. Make valley folds from the top corner to the upper corner of the feet, folding several layers at a time.

10. Fold the upper corner to the lower centre.

11. Shape the arms with valley creases from the outer corners to the inner folded edge.

12. Swing the pointed flap upwards to form the head.

13. Fold the top corner down (who wants a pointy head?) and widen the gap between the feet slightly.

14. Complete!

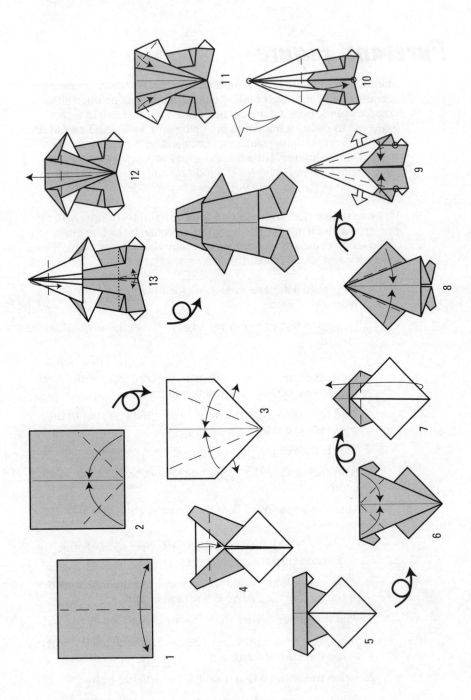

Sailboat Envelope

Michael LaFosse, from America, was commissioned to design this envelope by OrigamiUSA, because the traditional sailboat is their logo.

1. Start with a square, white side upwards. Fold in half from side to side, both ways.

2. Fold the lower edge and the right edge to meet the centre creases, and unfold again.

3. Turn the paper over and rotate slightly so a corner is towards you. (Curious how the square appears to be bigger than the previous drawing, even though it isn't.) Fold the lower corner to the centre, crease, and unfold.

4. Turn the paper over and fold the inner half of a diagonal by taking the bottom corner to the top, or vice-versa. This is a pre-crease which makes life easier in step 9.

5. Fold three corners in to the quarter creases.

6. Collapse the paper upwards as if it was a weird preliminary base. All the creases are in place for you.

7. Now you can see the little sailboat! Fold the base of the boat to the centre, crease, and unfold.

8. Turn the paper over from top to bottom. Fold the lower corner to the intersection of creases above it. Fold the upper corner over, reversing the crease you made in the step 7.

9. Fold the top section down on an existing crease.

10. Fold the left and right corners to meet at the centre.

11. Crease firmly and unfold.

12. Refold the same corners, but tuck them behind the sailboat.

13. Your envelope is ready to sail away.

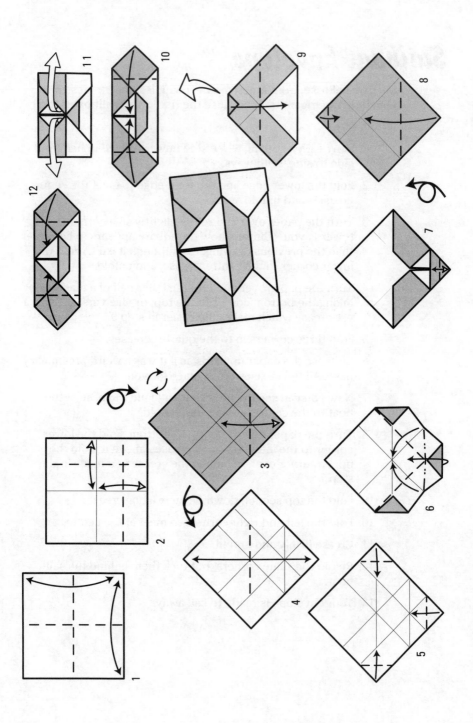

Dracula

Robin Glynn is an English creator who has a fascination with cartoon and fictional subjects. His work is rarely complex, but always cleverly thought out to put the right flaps in the right place.

Note the formation of the eyes by folding back a small corner to reveal the contrasting colour. There are many clever ways of achieving this; once you can see eyes, you quickly give clarity to the rest of the head.

1. Start with a square, white side upwards, with a corner towards you. Fold in half from corner to corner, then unfold both ways.

2. Fold left and right corners to the centre.

3. This is the result. Turn the paper over.

4. Fold left and right edges to the vertical centre, allowing the flaps to flip out from behind.

5. Fold top and bottom triangular flaps inwards.

6. Fold the same flaps over once more.

7. This is an enlarged view. Fold the left corner upwards at an angle to match the dotted profile.

8. Repeat on the right.

9. Fold the upper edge to lie on the white edge beneath it.

10. This is another enlarged view. Fold the coloured flaps inwards on the left and the right.

11. Fold two tips over to form the eyes.

12. Shape the head with four small mountain folds.

13. Your vampire is ready to bite!

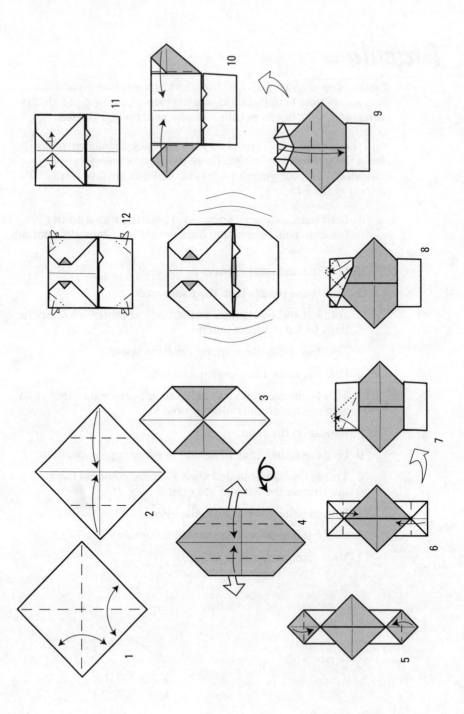

Lazy Winston

This design of mine is an Adaptation of a traditional design called the 'Lazy Susan' and I wondered how it would look folded from a hexagon rather than a square. Unexpectedly, the folding turned out to be simpler than from a square! Relatively few designs starting from a hexagon are simple – it's an inconvenient shape to create accurately. One of the simplest methods for creating the required 60-degree angle is to create a simple template, as shown in this sequence.

My model is named after an old college friend, who went by the glorious name of Winston N'Gobola.

1. Start with a square, creased on both diagonals and folded on one of them. Next fold the Elephant Head model (described earlier in this chapter) up to step 4. This is the template for getting an angle of 30 degrees. Overlap the two as shown.

2. Fold the lower flap over the template.

3. Remove the template and fold the left side to lie on the right side.

4. Crease the halfway vertical.

5. Fold the top section down, starting on the left where the raw edges end. Crease well and unfold.

6. Cut off the top section. Yes, cut! You could open out and fold over the surplus paper, but the end result isn't very attractive.

7. Open out to the hexagon. Fold three non-adjacent corners in to meet at the centre.

8. This is the result. Turn the paper over.

9. Fold each corner to the centre.

10. This is an enlarged view. This is the result. Turn the paper over.

11. Fold the paper in a similar way to if you were making a preliminary base. The upper right edge becomes an inside reverse.

12. Reinforce the vertical centre crease. Repeat on the underside.

13. Open out the first layer at the top, gently pressing in the centre of the folded edge at the bottom.

14. The paper forms into 3D. Repeat step 13 on the other two sides.

15. This is the completed model. You can use Lazy Winston to store almost anything from peanuts to sweets to small frogs.

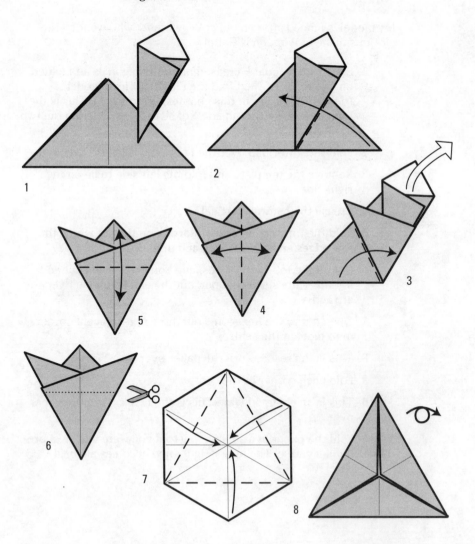

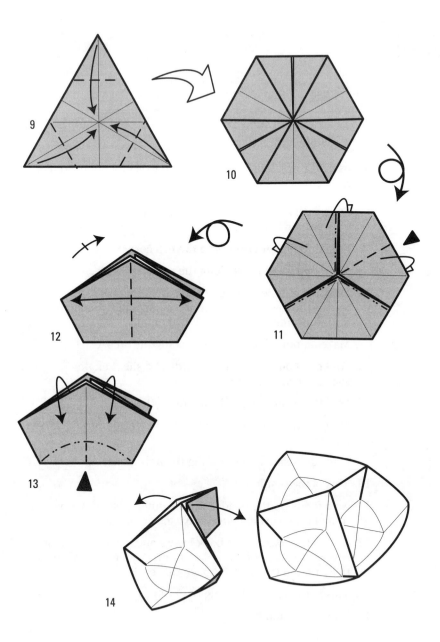

Hen

Tony O'Hare, from Wales, has been creating origami models for over thirty years and has created many classic designs along the way. Tony has the rare ability to produce a stylised but animated version of his chosen subject. This hen is a perfect example of using the paper economically to great effect.

The creases in steps four and six have no exact location, so use your judgement and fold them 'by eye'.

1. Start with a square, white side up, with the corner towards you. Fold in half from bottom to top.

2. Fold both lower corners to the top corner.

3. Mountain fold in half along the vertical centre.

4. Rotate the paper slightly to this position. Fold three-quarters of the lower edge over at a slight angle to match the dotted profile. Crease firmly and unfold.

5. Make an outside-reverse fold using the crease.

6. Fold both outer flaps backwards at a slight angle – check the next drawing for guidance.

7. Fold the front corners inside on both sides.

8. Fold the head flap over to match the dotted profile, crease, and unfold.

9. Make an inside-reverse using the new crease.

10. This is the result.

11. Now focus on the head. Fold the outer edge of the beak flap to meet the vertical edge, crease, and unfold.

12. Carefully separate the back layers and make an outside reverse fold on the outer layer only. You may need to partially unfold the beak to make this easier.

13. This is the result. Panning back, you get . . .

14. The completed hen.

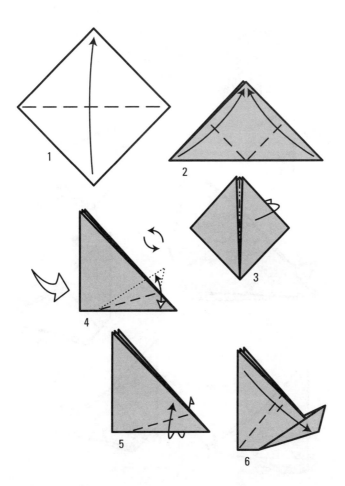

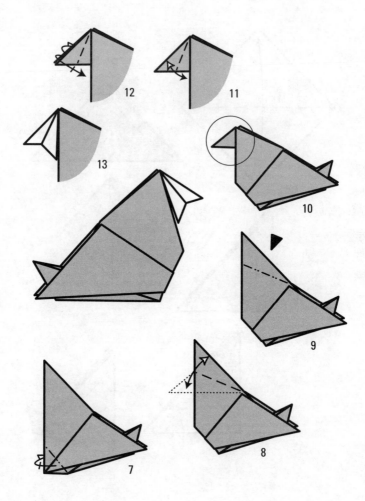

Chapter 5

Making Moderately Tricky Models

*I*f you've made the models in Chapter 4 you'll hopefully feel a little more confident when presented with an origami diagram. The designs in this chapter aren't a quantum leap upwards in complexity, so relax and enjoy them. I break down every step as usual, but refresh your memory in Chapters 1 and 2 for techniques if you need to.

Always look at the next drawing to see what you are aiming for. Sometimes you may reach the step without really knowing how; at which point unfold and refold to see how the drawing relates to the reality.

Read the text *before* you make the move, rather than using it in case of problems. However, if the diagrams alone are sufficient, that's fine, keep going!

Chair

John Montroll is one of the giants of American origami and his influence on origami as a whole is huge. John is known for complex designs, but as this design shows, he can turn his hand to simpler sequences as well. This chair is a neat and well-engineered model.

If you're feeling creative, a chair is a good subject to have a go at designing, and you can find many ingenious ways to achieve the required three dimensions. Or you might want to play about with expanding this design to make a settee.

1. Start with a square, coloured side up. Make a book-fold (fold in half from top to bottom, and from side to side) and unfold. Turn the paper over.

2. Fold left and right edges to the centre, crease, and unfold.

3. Fold left and right edges to the new creases.

4. Fold the lower edge to the centre.

5. Fold the short edge on both left and right over to lie on the horizontal edge, crease, and unfold.

6. Inside reverse both corners.

7. Fold the lower edge to the nearest edge.

8. Hold both loose flaps and fold them downwards. Now squash symmetrically the two coloured triangular flaps.

9. Make two creases that pass through the inside points of the coloured triangles.

10. Turn the paper over. Fold the lower edge to the upper edge, crease, and unfold.

11. Turn back over. Add these two valley folds. Try not to crease on the dotted lines, unless you simply can't avoid doing so.

12. Form the paper into 3D using the creases shown. The lower edge should end up at right angles to the upper section.

13. Keeping the paper 3D, turn the paper over. You'll need to hold the model in the air here. Lift the flap upwards, wrapping the sides around.

14. With a large slice of luck, this is what you'll see. Fold both sides to meet in the centre.

15. Shape the chair by folding a tiny corner over on either side.

16. Your chair is ready to sit on!

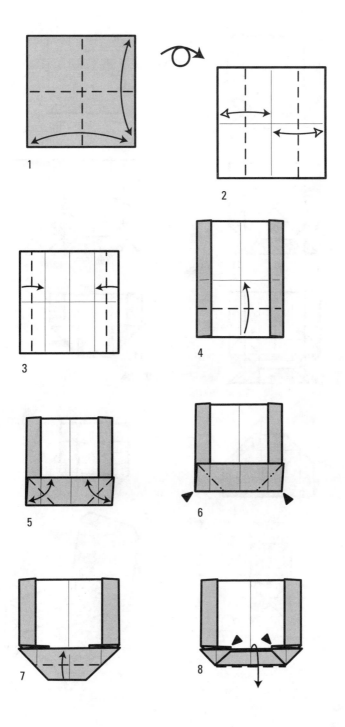

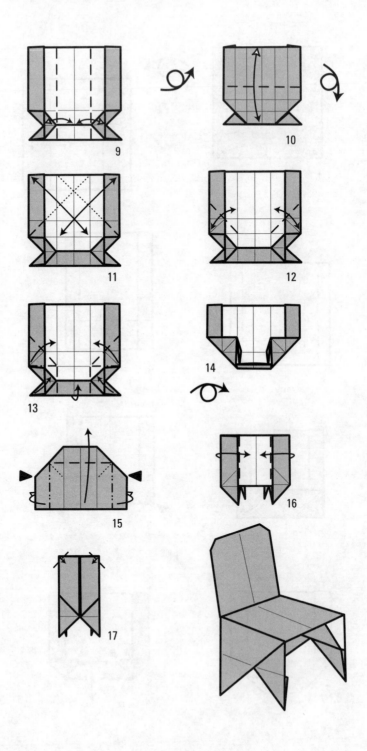

Jaws Fin

Many origami sharks are swimming about out there, but my design presents a shark as you might see it from a safe vantage point! Although the basic principle is straightforward, I've made sure that the base is neatly locked together.

When hunting for new subjects to create, try to think of unusual views and you'll realise that a rich seam of models is waiting to be discovered.

1. Start with a square, coloured side up, and crease a vertical diagonal.

2. Fold the lower corner to just short of the top corner. Anywhere close will do!

3. Fold the white corner to match the dotted line, crease, and unfold.

4. Repeat step 3 to the other side. Make sure the creases intersect.

5. Make a small rabbits ear in the centre (refer to Chapter 1).

6. Fold the small corners over on both sides.

7. Fold the coloured strips over the white edges, crease, and unfold.

8. Fold each half of the lower edge to lie on the vertical centre. Tuck one under the fin.

9. This is an optional step – you may like to add gentle creases to represent the wake of the fin in the water.

10. Turn the paper over. Fold the left and right corners in to meet the creases, crease, and unfold.

11. Make a horizontal pre-crease that passes through the intersection of creases at the top.

12. Form a preliminary base at the top, and inside reverse the left and right corners, tucking them between the layers underneath. Check the next drawing for guidance.

13. Fold over the flaps on either side, tucking them inside.

14. Turn the paper over for the finished shark!

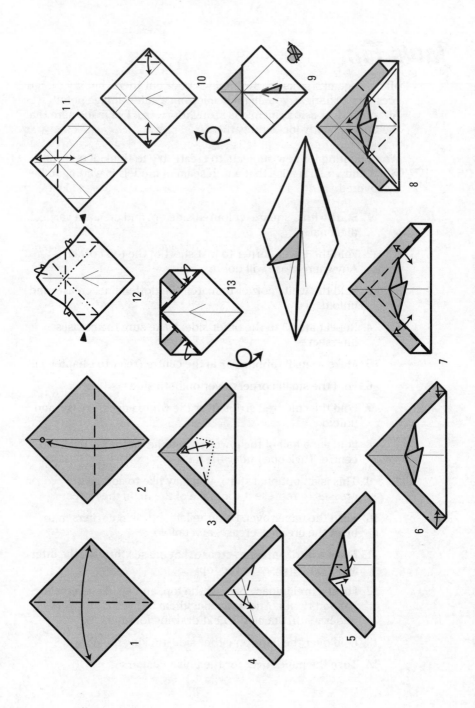

Boat

Here's a neat, three-dimensional rowing boat from Martin Wall with not one but three reverse folds for you to hone your abilities on. The design is beautifully thought through – every crease plays its part and is perfectly located. The final slightly curved shaping crease requires some practise but adds a touch of elegance to the finished model.

1. Start with a square, white side upwards. Crease in half from top to bottom.

2. Fold upper and lower edges to the centre, crease, and unfold.

3. Fold the lower corners together and make a very gentle pinch.

4. Fold the lower left corner to the pinchmark, make a firm crease, then unfold.

5. Fold the same edge to the new crease and unfold.

6. Fold the left hand corners over to lie along the quarter creases.

7. Fold in half upwards.

8. Fold the left and right lower edges to lie on the halfway crease, crease firmly, then unfold.

9. Neatly inside reverse both corners.

10. Inside reverse the upper edge on the right.

11. Repeat step 10 on the matching layers that are revealed.

12. Fold the top corner behind to lie on a raw edge.

13. Fold the upper layer inside, which should fit the gap!

14. Fold the top right corner over to meet the raw edge.

15. Fold the flap inside as you did in step 13.

16. Open the boat and add a gently curved crease if you're feeling confident!

17. Your boat is ready to set sail!

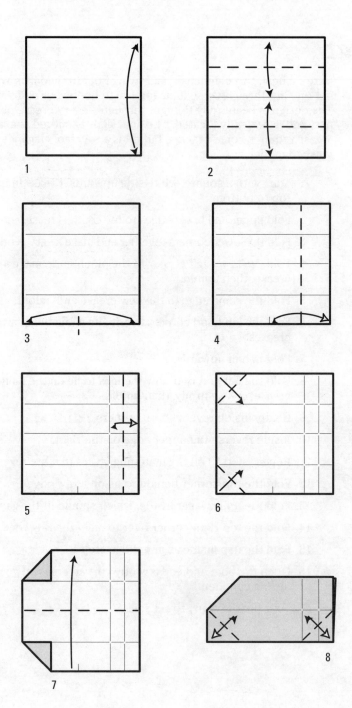

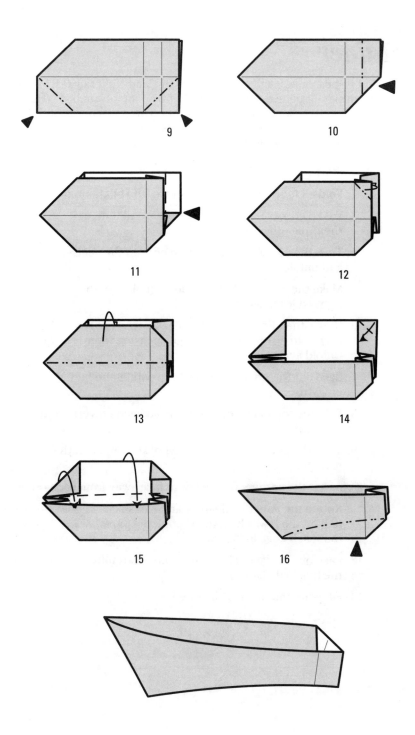

Container

I find dishes, boxes, and containers of any kind endlessly fascinating! This design of mine makes use of a blintzed multiform base (refer to Chapter 3) to lock the shape together. The container is perfect for storing all manner of useless objects to keep them just where they should be on your desk.

1. Start with an unfolded preliminary base.

2. Fold all four corners to the centre (the blintzing).

3. Fold a corner to the centre, crease, and unfold. Repeat with the three other corners.

4. Turn the paper over. Fold each edge to the centre, crease, and unfold.

5. Make the creases shown – the midpoints of the left and right edges meet at the centre.

6. Here's the blintzed multiform base. Fold the lower right corner to lie on the lower edge, creasing where shown. Unfold again.

7. Ease out the original corner from within and fold it upwards.

8. Fold the top back down, making an inside reverse fold on the right.

9. Tuck the outer corner into the pocket, underneath the reversed layers.

10. Swing the corners on the left to face away from each other.

11. Rotate the paper 90 degrees anti-clockwise. Repeat steps 6 to 9 on the lower half, then rotate the paper twice more so that each edge is the same.

12. Ease out the layers from the centre, carefully pinching into the finished shape.

13. Fill your container with sweeties.

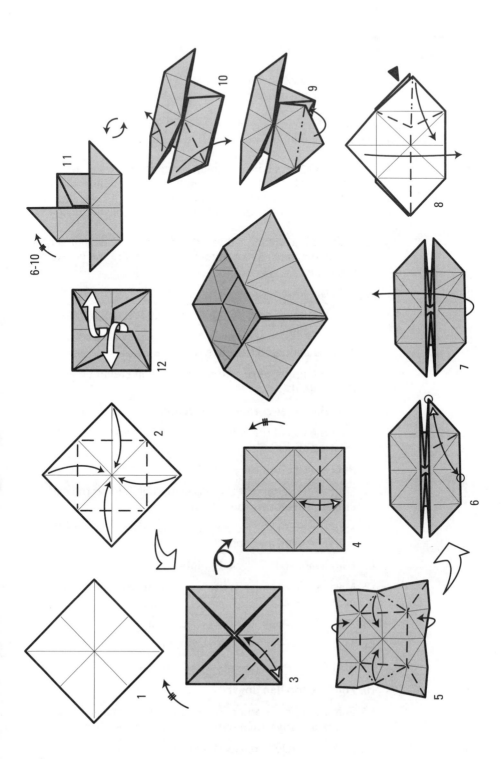

Face Envelope

One of the delights of being in contact with other folders is that you get wonderful surprises through the post. Many folders are fans of origami envelopes, such as Michel Grand of France. This design arrived through my letterbox as *Origami Kit For Dummies* was nearing completion, but I just had to include it.

As an extra challenge, I had no folding sequence for it, so I devised it by carefully unfolding and re-folding until I worked out how the model came together. This 'backwards' technique is called *reverse engineering* and is almost as much fun as folding the more conventional way.

1. Start with a square, white side upwards, creased on a horizontal diagonal. Make a small pinch to mark the centre of the paper.

2. Fold the lower corner to the centre.

3. Fold the lower edge to the centre, crease, and unfold back to the square.

4. Add a diagonal to the lower quarter.

5. Fold the upper corner to meet the most recent crease, then unfold.

6. Fold the lower corner to the centre.

7. Fold the top of the coloured triangular flap to meet the existing crease.

8. Repeat step 7 on the right side.

9. Fold a tiny section at the top over, then fold on the existing crease. This forms the mouth.

10. Fold the outer circled points to the centre circle, crease where shown, and unfold.

11. Fold again so the circled points meet.

12. Make a squash fold on the left, forming the short valley crease as you flatten.

13. This is the result. Repeat on the right.

14. Make these pre-creases through both layers.

15. Add two vertical creases where shown.

16. Fold the top flap down.

17. Fold the upper corners over (the creases are on the lower layers already), then unfold. Fold the corner back up again.

18. Make an angled crease as shown.

19. Tuck the corner of the eye behind, and repeat steps 17 and 18 on the left.

20. Collapse the top edge down using existing creases. (It doesn't matter which layer lies under which.)

21. Tuck the point at the bottom into a pocket just above the mouth.

22. Complete.

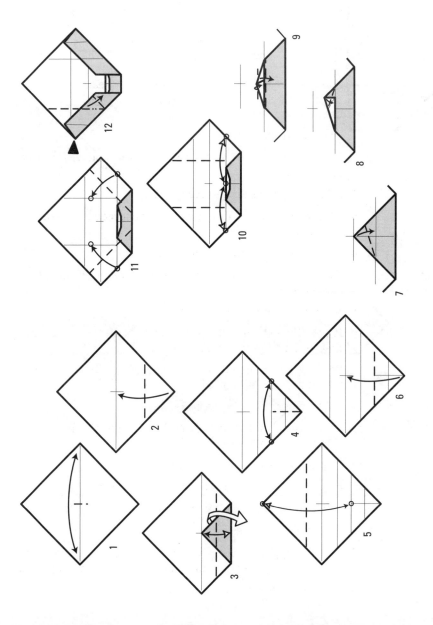

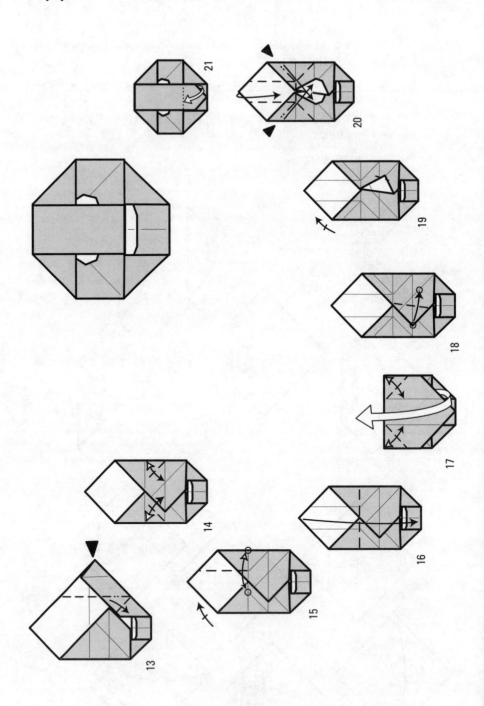

Mystery Object

Sometimes you create a design that doesn't appear to have a purpose in life. You like the folding sequence and it appears to be something, but you don't know what. A little consideration and the true
genius of the design makes itself apparent. If not, simply ask another
folder what your model is – he or she may provide an inspired
answer, whereupon you enthusiastically say 'Got it in one!'.

This design of mine is the kind of practical tool that nobody should
be without. If you can't work out what it is, turn to the end of the
chapter.

1. Start with a square, coloured side upwards, creased along a
   vertical diagonal. Fold the lower sides to the centre.

2. Turn the paper over. Fold the upper triangular flap
   downwards.

3. This is the result. Turn the paper over.

4. Fold the lower edges to the vertical centre but stop as they
   reach the hidden edge underneath.

5. Join the end of these creases to the upper corners, creasing along the hidden edge.

6. Make a third crease from the top centre to the intersection of
   the last two creases. This needs some care to fold properly.

7. Open the right-hand flap out.

8. Fold the left side over on the vertical centre crease.

9. Fold the right-hand flap back over, tucking it under the
   coloured triangular flap.

10. Carefully make the paper 3D using the creases shown to
    achieve the final shape.

11. The mystery object is complete. Can you tell what you can
    use it for?

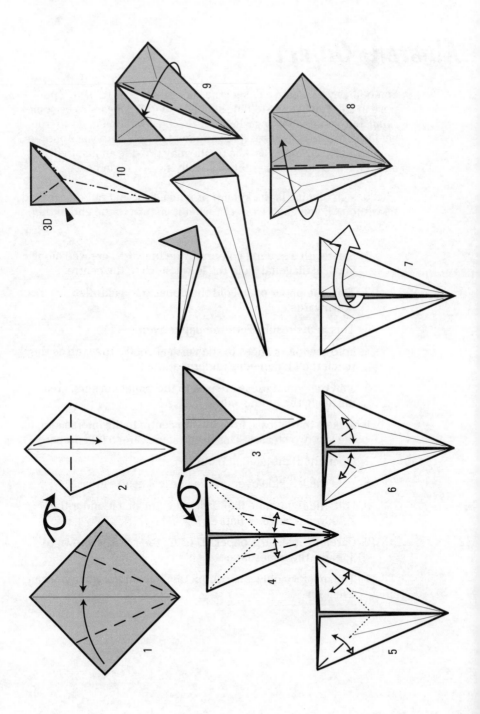

Bluebell

This traditional design is one of the earliest examples of a technique that has come to be known as a *butterfly lock*. The lock works by crimping one layer over another, then folding it back in half so a part of the paper is trapped inside, making it perfect for containers and 3D forms. You can see it taking place in steps 8 and 9.

The completed model makes a fine flower or, hung upside-down, a bell for a Christmas tree.

1. Start with a square, coloured side upwards and add both diagonal creases.
2. Fold all four corners to the centre.
3. Make a fold that passes through the centre of the paper. When in place, the lower-right centre point needs to lie on the vertical centre.
4. This is the result. Crease firmly and unfold.
5. The creases should look like this. Check that your creases match the figure before proceeding!
6. Rotate the paper 90 degrees and repeat step 5.
7. Unfold all four corners.
8. Alter the indicated creases to become valleys.
9. Form the paper into 3D using the creases shown.
10. Fold the corner down, flattening on existing creases.
11. Here the move is shown from a different angle.
12. Now you're back to the view in step 10. Moving anti-clockwise, repeat step 9 on the next section.
13. Fold the corner in to lock it.
14. Repeat the lock on the remaining two corners.
15. Your bluebell is complete.

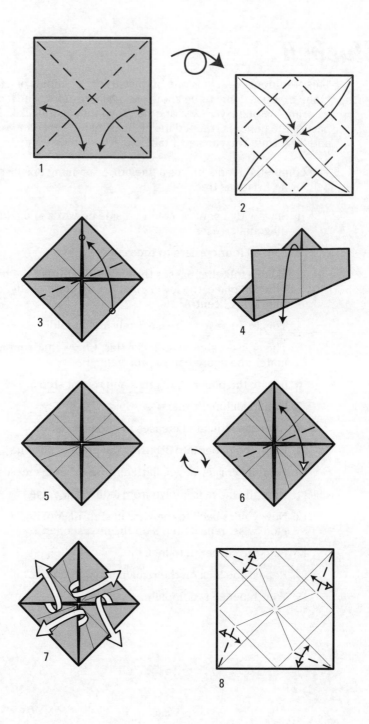

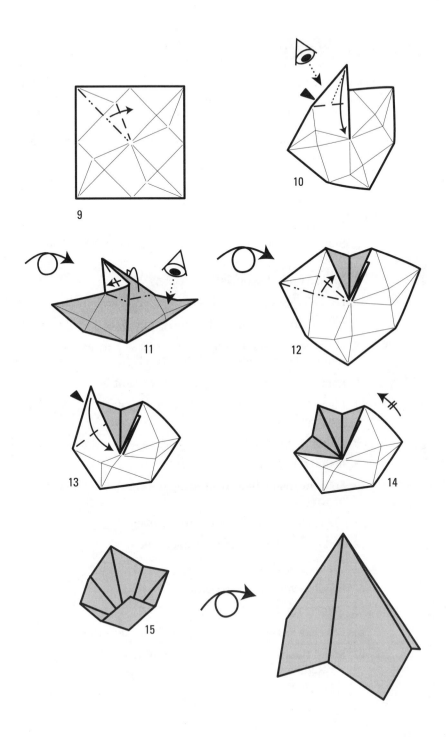

Shining Heart

The layers of an origami model have an unexpected bonus in that they let through different amounts of light, depending on how many layers there are. You can use this to create simple silhouettes. This design of mine is based on work by Wayne Brown, who in turn based his model on work by Stephen Palmer! Such is the way with origami – one idea inspires another and you try to acknowledge the influences where you can.

Think of other shapes you can produce using the same idea of layering.

1. Start with a square, coloured side upwards. Book fold in half both ways.

2. Crease both diagonals.

3. Fold all four edges to the centre, crease, and unfold.

4. Fold all four corners to the nearest intersection of creases.

5. Fold the corners over again on a crease between the midpoints of each edge.

6. Fold the left and right corners to the centre.

7. Pleat the triangular flaps into equal thirds, or as close as you can guess.

8. Unfold steps 6 and 7.

9. Inside reverse the two corners.

10. Fold the inside flaps over using the creases you made in step 7.

11. This is the result. Turn the paper over.

12. Make a small pleat on the top corner.

13. Unfold the pleat.

14. Inside reverse the top corner.

15. Reform the peat at the top.

16. Fold the lower corner behind at 90 degrees to form a stand.

17. Stand the heart in front of a window and let the sun shine through!

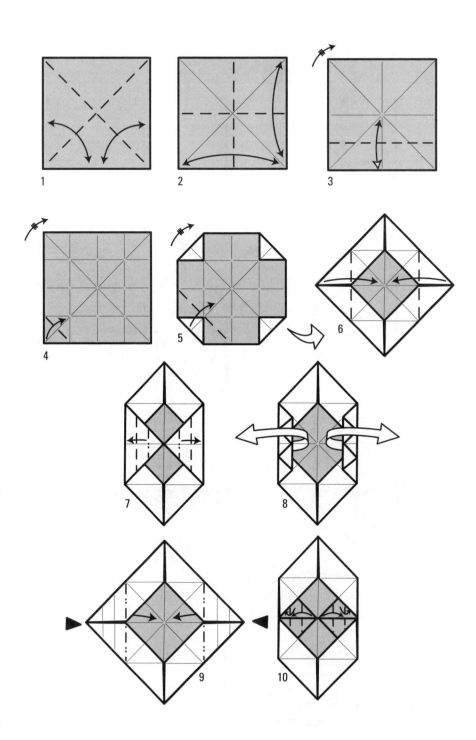

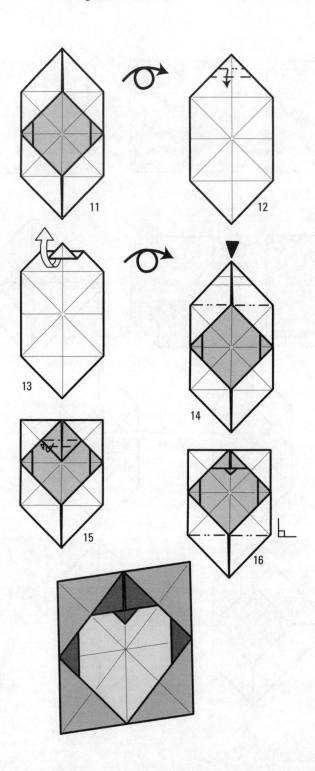

11

12

13

14

15

16

Tulip Bowl

This model is a classic example of how a few carefully chosen creases can create a form with beauty that holds its shape with no seeming effort. Peter Borcherds has his own style and comes up with small but meaningful contributions to origami. One such example is shown here in the use of *templates*.

Many times in origami, creases are put into the paper simply to locate other creases and once this is achieved, they're redundant. In this model, you need a vertical halfway crease in order to create a 60-degree crease. Rather than folding it, you make a simple template from another identical square and use that to locate the crease. The end result is a model with functionally minimal creases.

1. Start with a square the same size that you want your model to be. Fold it in half.

2. Place the sheet that will produce the model inside the template sheet as far as it will go.

3. Starting the crease at the lower left corner, fold the lower right corner up until it lies on the edge of the template.

4. Make a crease about two-thirds of the way from the left-hand corner.

5. This is the result.

6. Rotate the paper 90 degrees anti-clockwise and repeat the fold in step 4. Continue with the remaining two corners.

7. You should now have these creases in place. Turn the paper over.

8. Again starting the crease at the lower left corner, fold the lower edge to lie on the existing crease. Only make that section of the crease that extends out to the edge from the nearest crease.

9. You should now have these creases. Turn the paper over.

10. Make the paper 3D using two creases.

11. Repeat step 10 moving clockwise . . .

12. . . . and again . . .

13. . . . and with the final set.

14. This is the view from above.

15. Your finished tulip bowl.

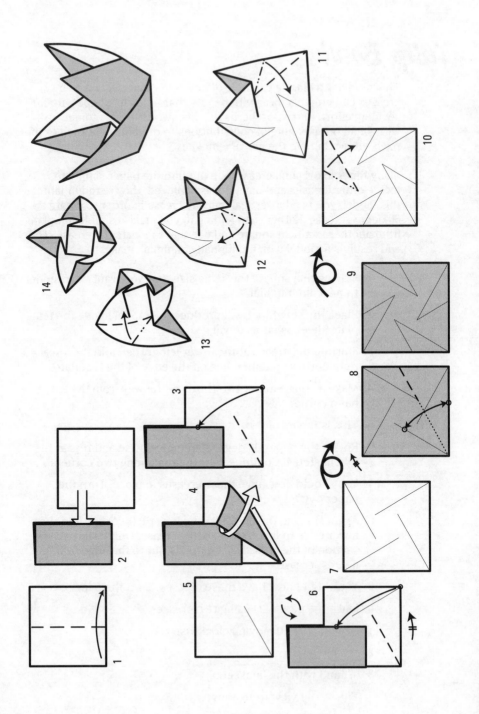

Little Nicky

I created this design many years ago and named it after my young son, who was around 3 at the time and excessively cute. He's now 21, over 6 feet tall, with long hair and the requisite tattoo, and is a drummer in a melodic death metal band. Ah, the delights of parenthood.

As with all planes, you can experiment with the angles of the wings and speed of launching to find the optimum launching technique. Every plane has an optimum configuration and it may not be the first one you try, so persevere.

1. Start with a square, coloured side up. Make a vertical book fold.

2. Fold the left and right edges to the centre, crease, and unfold.

3. Fold both lower corners so that the crease starts in the centre and the outer corners lie on the quarter creases. This produces the required 60-degree angle.

4. This is the result. Turn the paper over.

5. Fold the lower edges to lie on the vertical centre.

6. This is the result. Turn the paper over.

7. Fold the lower corner to the centre of the upper edge.

8. This is what it should look like so far.

9. Turn back over and fold each half of the lower edge to the vertical centre.

10. Turn over once more (getting dizzy?).

11. Open and squash the central pocket downwards.

12. Fold a triangular section underneath at the lower end.

13. Fold in half from right to left.

14. Fold the tips of both wings over to meet the nearest crease.

15. Fold the body in half, so that the circled point on the left meets the vertical right edge. Turn the paper over and repeat (or it really wouldn't fly very well!).

16. Unfold the wings and wingtips to match the profile of the final drawing.

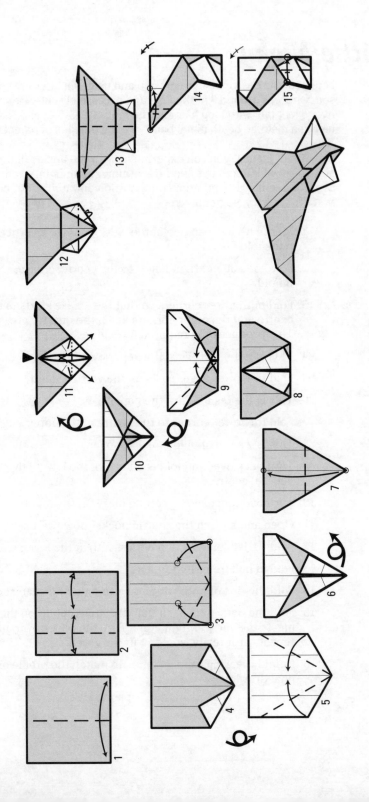

Makotokoma (Spinning Top)

You might think a spinning top to be a trivial achievement in origami, but this is not the case. Making a device that's rigid enough to be rapidly spun and has the appropriate weight distribution is a real challenge. Makoto Yamaguchi is one of the most experienced origami creators in Japan. He formed the Japanese Origami Academic Society (JOAS), a group responsible for much of the complex origami that has emerged from Japan in recent years.

In this design you use three simple elements to combine into the top.

Base

1. Start with a square, white side upwards, and crease both diagonals.

2. Turn the paper over and book-fold in half twice.

3. Turn back over and fold all four corners to the centre.

4. This is the starting point for all the sections of the top.

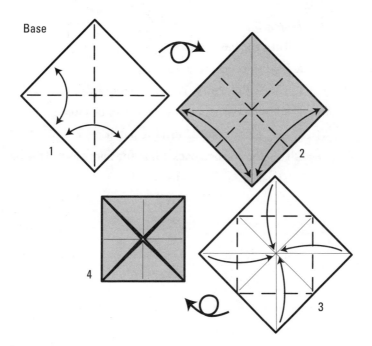

Base

Outer section

1. Fold all four corners to the centre.
2. Fold the corners back out to the midpoints of the outer edges.
3. The section complete.

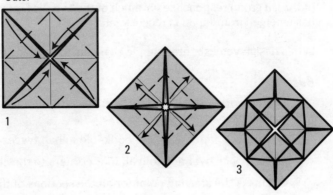

Outer

1

2

3

Middle section

1. Turn the base over.
2. Fold the corners to the centre.
3. This is the result. Turn the paper over.
4. Fold the corners to the centre once more.
5. This is the result. Turn the paper over.
6. Fold the corners back out to the midpoints of the outer edges.
7. The section complete.

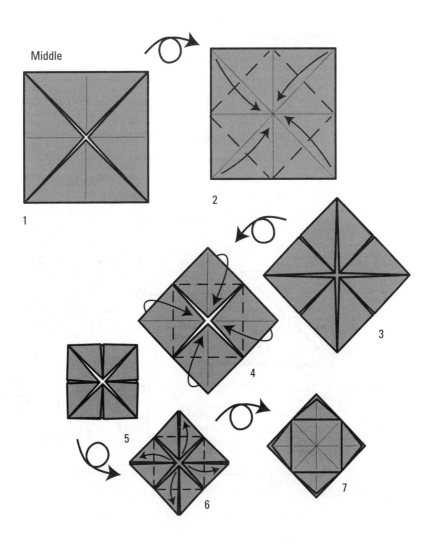

Middle

Inner section

1. Fold four corners to the centre.

2. This is the result. Turn the paper over.

3. Fold four corners to the centre. You should be good at this by now!

4. This is an enlarged view. Book-fold in half both ways.

5. Turn the paper over and crease both diagonals.

6. Collapse the paper into a water-bomb base (Chapter 3 describes the waterbomb base).

7. The section complete.

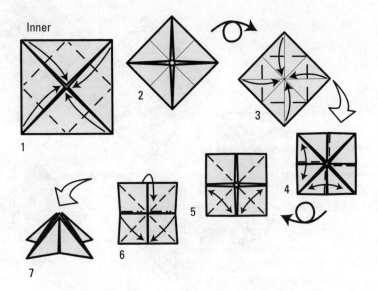

Assembly

1. Take the outer section and unfold the outer flaps.

2. Place the middle section in the centre of the paper.

3. Refold the flaps, tucking them under the upper corners.

4. Slightly open a pocket on each side.

5. Slide the inner section into the pockets.

6. Take the model for a spin!

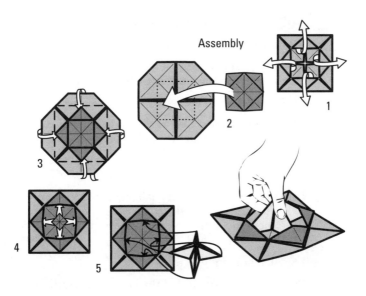

Flood Bowl

This is one of the many bowls I've created. When you design lots of bowls and dishes, naming them becomes a problem. I gave up numbering at Dish 22 and started to assign names based on things that were happening in my life instead. At the time I finished this bowl, my home town of Sheffield was being devastated by extraordinary floods, hence the name.

The geometry of this model is that of the kite base (refer to Chapter 3) and the interesting move at step 11 produces a small kite shape, used to hold the model together.

1. Start with a square, coloured side up, and crease along the vertical diagonal. Fold the lower edges to the vertical centre, crease, and unfold.

2. Rotate the paper 180 degrees and repeat step 1.

3. Turn the paper over. Using the reference points on the right, add a crease at right angles to the lower left edge. Don't crease on the dotted line.

4. Repeat step 3 on the left, then twice more at the opposite end.

5. Turn the paper over. Form a horizontal crease by folding so the circled areas meet up. Repeat at the other end.

6. Do another pre-crease, carefully noting the location points.

7. Refold the kite base and turn the paper over.

8. This is an enlarged view. Fold the small horizontal valley, then unfold the kite base from beneath.

9. Change the creases where shown to become valleys.

10. Make a valley crease through the intersection points. The lower edge meets the circled point.

11. Rotate the paper 180 degrees, to make folding easier. Fold the sides underneath on existing creases.

12. This step is a bit of a challenge. Fold the white edges on the valley creases. At the same time open out the paper on either side at the top and aim to form a small coloured kite shape. Persevere!

13. This, hopefully, is the result.

14. Tuck the lower end of the kite underneath to hold the paper in place.

15. Repeat steps 10 to 15 on the opposite side.

16. Here's the completed flood bowl. Give yourself a pat on the back and have a biscuit!

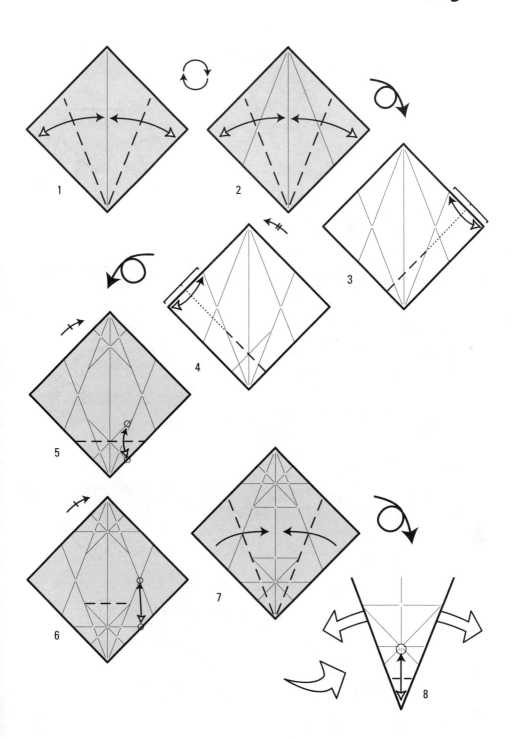

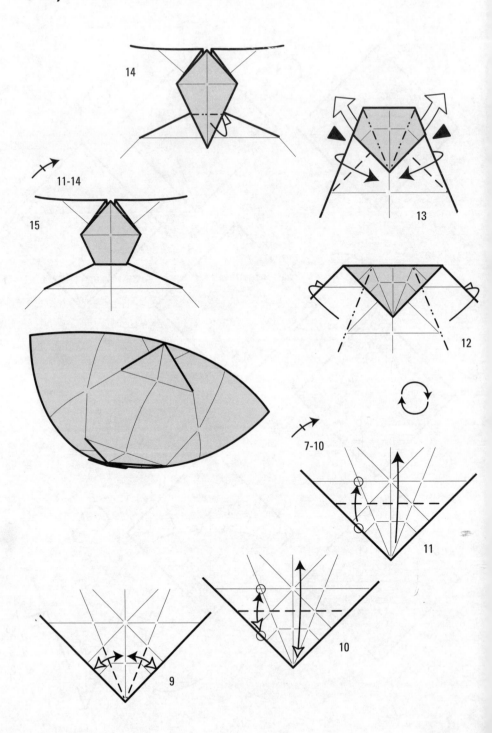

Flapping Bird

I couldn't attempt to show you what origami is about without including this classic. A recent survey of keen paperfolders rated this flapping bird in the top three designs of all time. It's a relatively simple traditional model, yet guaranteed to delight anyone with an ounce of fun inside them. Children love it. Technically, the model is a simple development of the bird base.

Making the critter start to fly is the trickiest part. Ease the tail out and mutter words of encouragement. After the bird has made the first flap, it should perform without problems.

1. Start with a bird base (surprise, surprise). Fold the upper and lower flaps upwards.

2. Fold the upper left flap to the right, turn the paper over, and do the same on that side.

3. Fold both flaps upwards again.

4. Hold the inner flap and ease it out to match the dotted line. Flatten the paper along the lower edge so it stays in place.

5. Repeat step 4 with the central flap on the left.

6. Decide the point to be the beak (choose the neatest point!) and fold it over into a suitable position. Crease and unfold.

7. Inside reverse the beak.

8. *Gently* curl the paper along the dotted line to help the bird fly. Don't put in a firm crease.

9. Hold at the circled areas and gently ease the tail in the direction of the arrow, then relax.

10. Your bird can fly away!

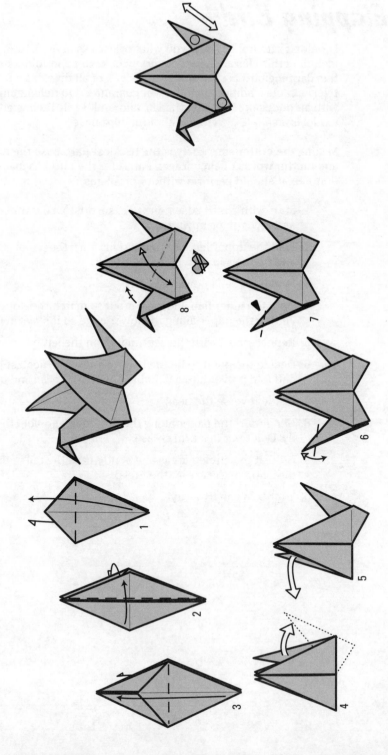

Droodle

I recently discovered the work of American humorist Roger Price who, in the 1950s, invented a genre of cartoon called a droodle (a drawing meets a doodle, presumably?). They show highly simplified sketches of something that puzzles people, yet is strikingly obvious once you read the caption and know what it is. I was intrigued by Price's work and developed several origami versions of his ideas. It was an interesting creative challenge to come up with the model you see here. I explain a little of the geometry, but you can skip past it if it frightens you.

1. Start with a square, white side upwards, creased in half on the horizontal. Fold each lower half of the left and right edges to the crease. Crease and unfold.

2. Starting at the right centre, fold the lower left corner so that the 45-degree crease lies on the horizontal crease. Only crease in the right quarter. (This creates an angle of 67.5 degrees, maths fans!)

3. Starting the crease at the centre of the right-hand vertical edge, fold the lower half of the right edge to meet the most recent crease, pinching the lower edge only. This makes an angle of 33.75 degrees, which (for our purposes) divides the lower edge into thirds. Are you impressed?

4. Fold the lower right corner to meet this latest pinch, crease, and unfold a vertical one-sixth crease.

5. Fold the lower edge to where the last crease meets the 45-degree crease.

6. Fold so that the most recent crease lies on the halfway crease. This marks the lower third of the vertical edge.

7. Turn the paper over. Add a one-sixth crease on the right, and a one-third crease on the left.

8. Turn back over and form an inside reverse fold.

9. Fold the left edge to the centre, crease, and unfold.

10. Fold a couple more pre-creases, as shown. Note the locations carefully.

11. Make a squash fold on the lower left, and yet another pre-crease at the top right.

12. On the right, make a crease that joins the circled points. Add a small pre-crease to the triangular area.

13. Fold the triangular flap to the right. Fold over the tiny upper right corner.

14. Fold the lower point over and down, squashing so that the tip points vertically down.

15. Tuck the white flap behind.

16. Swing the lower coloured flap upwards.

17. Refold the angled crease on the right so it passes through the coloured layers. Fold the whole flap back down again.

18. Fold the left edge over on the second vertical crease from the left.

19. Fold the lower section upwards again.

20. Fold the left-hand edge behind on an existing crease. Fold the paper behind on the angled crease (taking a hidden layer with it). Fold the top corner over and back. Phew!

21. Fold the top coloured edge inside, making a squash fold at the corner.

22. Fold the right-hand edge behind.

23. So, after all that, what on earth is it? If you can't guess, turn to the end of the chapter for the answer.

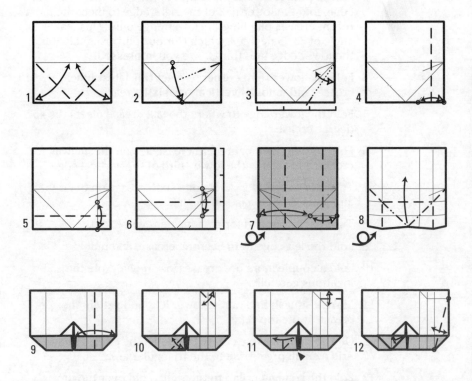

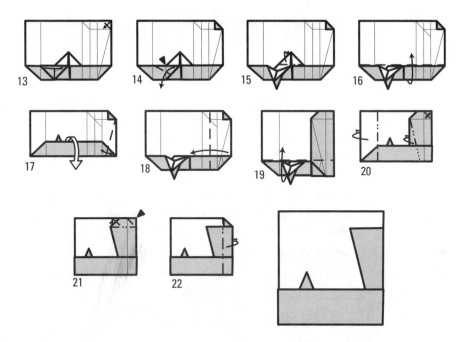

Vase

If you are of a creative bent, as you fold a design you may have ideas for further developing or adapting it. Gay Merrill Gross includes the following statement with her diagrams: 'This is a hybrid model, combining the folding pattern of Aldo Putignano's 4-Step Vase, with the pot-bellied shape of Toshie Takahama's Vase.' By doing this Gay not only offers a superb design, but gives the sources to investigate to see how she developed the ideas. Doing so is simultaneously respecting the past and offering something for the future.

Make sure you concentrate during the sequence to ensure that you alternate the flaps properly. The model has *rotational symmetry*; in other words, it looks the same whichever way you look at it if you arrange the layers evenly on any of the sides.

1. Start with a preliminary base, colour out. Fold over a small section at the closed corner. This determines the size of the base.

2. Sink the point.

3. Starting at the edge of the base, fold the first right-hand corner to meet the vertical centre.

4. Turn over the paper and repeat the move.

5. Fold the right-hand layers to the left, turn the paper over, and repeat on the opposite side.

6. Repeat step 3 on the front and back.

7. Fold the upper triangular flap down. Repeat this move on each of the matching flaps.

8. Unfold the upper flap.

9. Fold the upper right edge to lie on the vertical centre.

10. Fold the top corner down again.

11. Unfold the flaps from underneath.

12. Do a minor miracle, as you did in step 5.

13. Repeat steps 8 to 11 on each side, leaving the final folds in place.

14. Fold the flaps to the right, front, and back.

15. Refold the flap inside. Rotate the flaps again and repeat.

16. Here's the final corner being completed.

17. Carefully open the vase from inside, pressing it into shape.

18. Your vase is complete!

As a variation, you can fold the white flap underneath before opening.

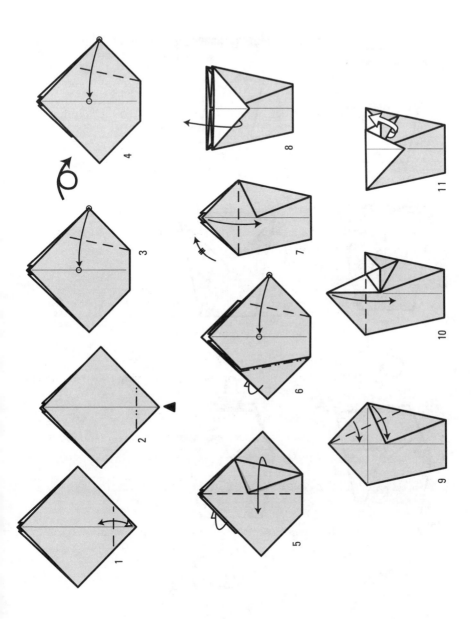

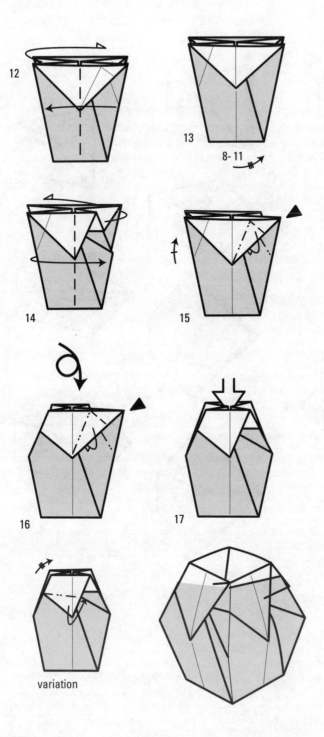

12

13

8-11

14

15

16

17

variation

Hearts

Origami designs usually represent a single figure. To achieve a double object without excessive complexity requires both ingenuity and imagination. The late Eric Kenneway, who designed this Hearts model, had a unique style and produced many hundreds of designs but, being a shy figure, his work wasn't widely available, especially in the days before the Internet.

1. Start with a square, white side upwards. Book-fold in half both ways.

2. Fold the upper and lower edges to the centre, crease, and unfold.

3. Fold the upper and lower edges to the opposite three-quarter crease, but only crease half the paper.

4. Mountain fold the bottom half underneath.

5. Fold the lower left corner to the halfway crease, crease firmly, and unfold.

6. Fold the same edge to the new crease, crease and unfold.

7. Turn the paper over and repeat steps 5 and 6 before unfolding fully.

8. Fold all four corners to lie on the quarter creases.

9. This is the result. Turn the paper over.

10. Starting at the corner shown, fold so that the two adjacent edges line up. This makes a crease that bisects the angle of the corner. Repeat on the opposite side.

11. Mountain fold the right half behind.

12. Make a small 45-degree crease. Turn over and repeat on the other side.

13. The creases you've just made need to be mountain on both sides. Start to gently press in the centre of the top edge, as you make the vertical folds on both sides at once.

14. This is the move in progress.

    The move is happening on both sides, in mirror image.

15. If you've come this far, congratulations! Unfold and refold until you have a fair idea of what you've done with the paper. Now hold the paper in both hands by the circled areas and twist the left half downwards slightly. You're trying to persuade the paper to fold along the hidden creases shown by the dotted lines.

16. This should be the result. Fold the corner behind.

17. Fold the same flap behind again. Repeat both folds on the under

18. Inside reverse the two right-angled corners.

19. Gently form the model into 3D.

20. Your model is complete.

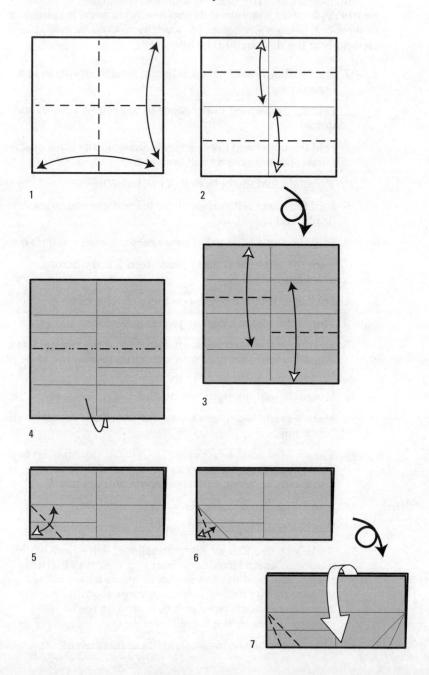

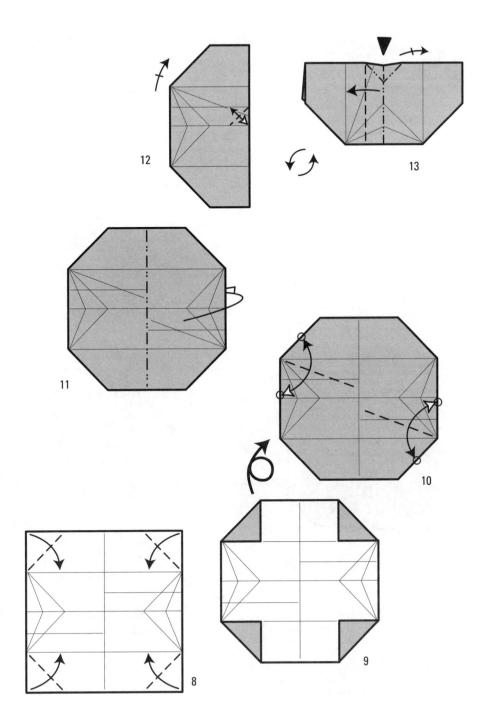

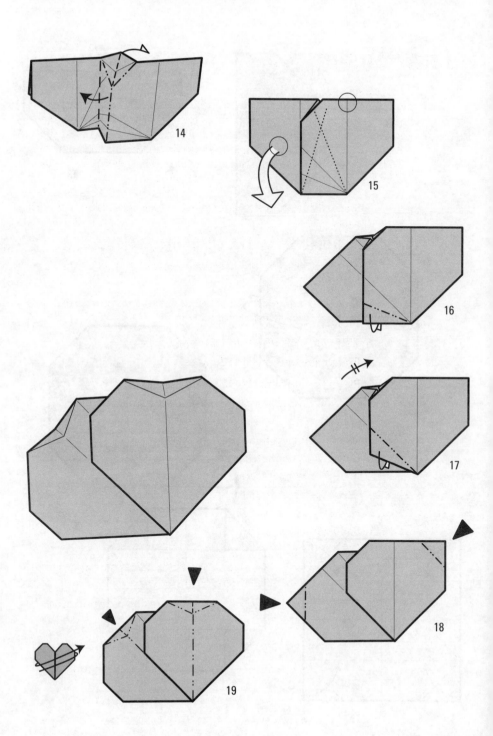

Lazy Susan

Lazy Susan is one of the few designs in the world of origami that's circular when finished. The wonderful sequence produces a surprising result. The design originates from the Szechwan province in Western China, where the five compartments represent the five happinesses (health, wealth, longevity, virtue, and natural death). To bring this list up to date, I'd add a sixth happiness: a fast, reliable Internet connection.

1. Start with a square, coloured side up. Book-fold in half both ways.

2. Turn the paper over and neatly crease both diagonals.

3. Turn back over and fold all four corners to the centre (a blintz).

4. This is an enlarged view. Fold the central corners back out to the midpoints of the outer edges.

5. This is the result. Turn the paper over.

6. Pre-crease four quarter creases.

7. Pinch the corners together and outline the central square.

8. Form a waterbomb base in the centre of the paper as you gently collapse the paper.

9. This should be the result. As always, I recommend that you unfold and refold the paper so you understand what's happened. Inside reverse the left point.

10. This is the result. Repeat on the right and twice on the lower side.

11. Slide a finger into the first pocket and carefully press down the white folded edge so that it becomes a curved crease.

12. This is what you're aiming at. Try to make the crease symmetrical. Repeat on the other three sides.

13. Turn the paper over for the completed Lazy Susan!

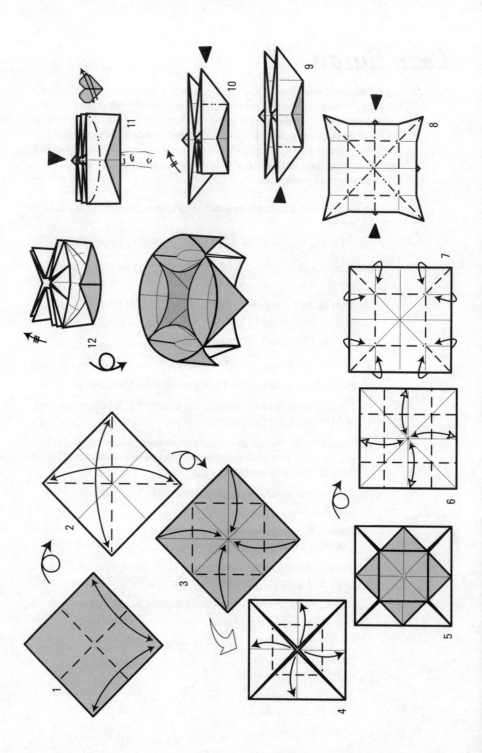

Four Thirsty Birds

Some folders can spend half their lifetime being an origami enthusiast and rarely yet create. David Lister of Grimsby, England, is one such folder. David is world-famous as one of the leading experts in origami history, yet his own creations come along with every second pass of Halley's Comet. However, they're well worth waiting for, as this design shows.

David developed the corners of the bowl to form birds. The finished result has charm and grace.

1. Start with a square, coloured side upwards, and add both diagonal creases.

2. Fold a corner to the centre, crease, and unfold. Repeat on the three other corners.

3. Fold the lower edge to the centre (there are three location points). Repeat on the three other corners.

4. Collapse one corner into a preliminary base form.

5. Repeat on the three other corners. (This is the windmill or multiform base.)

6. Fold the edges of one corner square to the diagonal, crease, and unfold. Repeat on the three other corners.

7. Inside reverse both edges of the square section. Repeat on the three other corners. (You are, in effect, forming one wing of a bird base.)

8. Fold all four pointed ends outwards.

9. Fold the inner corner downwards, approximately two-thirds of the way down. If you're not good with thirds, err towards a higher crease rather than a lower one.

10. Fold the corner back up to the white edge.

11. Fold the double layer over and tuck it underneath. Repeat on the three other corners.

12. Fold a pointed flap to the centre. Repeat on the other three corners.

13. Fold the outer edges of the diamond shape to the centre. Repeat on the three other corners.

14. Pinch the outer edges of the birds together, gently forming a bowl in the centre. Don't over-sharpen the inner bowl creases.

15. Make a typical beak fold, inside reversing the ends of each pointed flap.

16. Your birds are ready to drink.

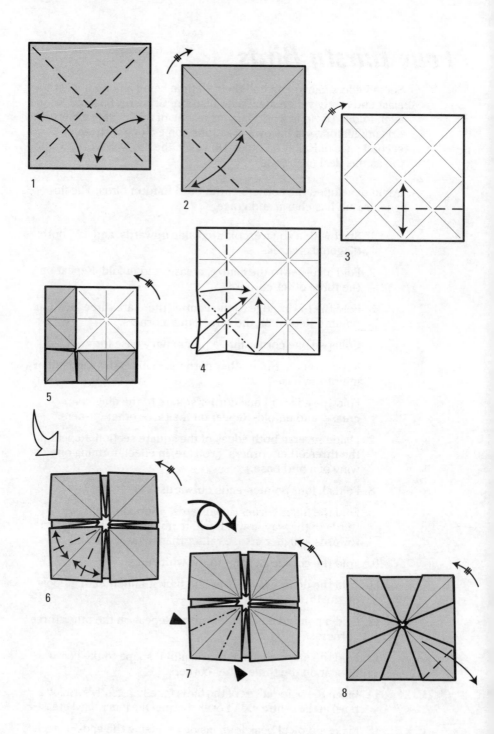

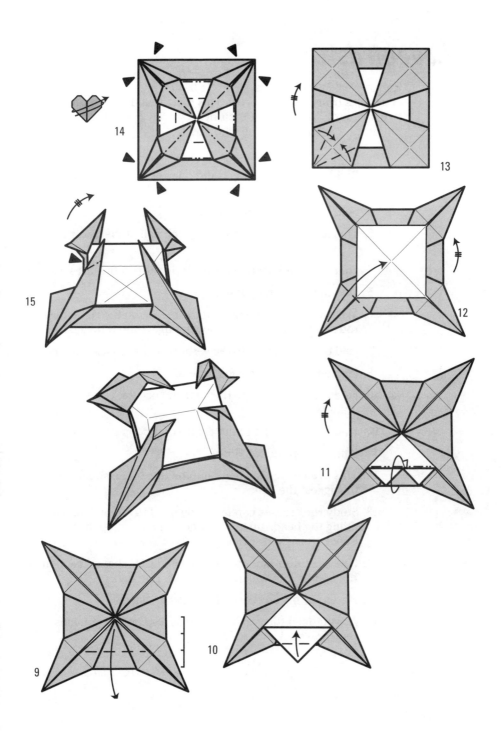

Lovebirds

Robert Neale is an origami giant. He has an inventive mind and can see things from unusual angles. This delightful design represents two lovebirds who pop out their heads to say hello. The action is unique and enchanting to all who see it.

1. Start with a 2 by 1 rectangle (half a square), white side up. Divide in half both ways, add quarter creases in both halves, and eighth creases in the top half.

2. Fold in half from top to bottom.

3. This is an enlarged view. Fold each half of the lower edge to the vertical centre.

4. Fold the lower section upwards on the existing crease.

5. Fold in half from right to left.

6. Make a crease running from the crease on the right edge to roughly the middle of the lower edge. Unfold the last step.

7. Fold the outer edges to the vertical crease, crease, and unfold.

8. Inside reverse the same corners.

9. Fold the top corner to the nearest corners, crease, and unfold.

10. Fold three corners to the centre of the top section.

11. Fold the top section down.

12. This is an enlarged view. Fold the tips of the squares over to suggest the hair.

13. Study the creases carefully. You need to fold in half while lifting the heads up in the middle and opening them out. Check the next drawing.

14. Fold the lower half upwards, forming a V-shaped section in the middle into which the head section tucks.

15. Flatten firmly so everything stays in place.

16. As you open the paper, the heads pop out; as you close, they pop back.

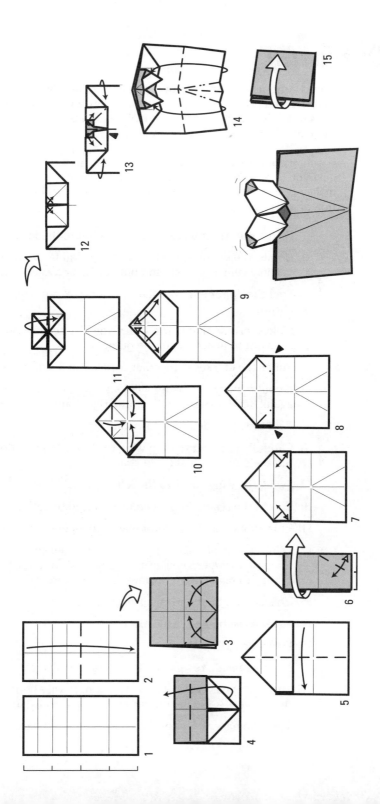

Dragonfly

Anita Barbour is a creator with a true style of her own. She creates simple to intermediate designs that have real charm and she seems to find subjects to fold that others don't think of. Several origami dragonflies are out there, but this is far and away my favourite.

Forming the eyes may cause you a little difficulty to start with, so I suggest you fold from a larger sheet of paper than usual, until the moves make sense. Even without the eyes, the model is still a fine representation of a dragonfly.

1. Fold a waterbomb base with the colour outside.

2. Rotate 180 degrees. Fold the left edge (all layers together) to the vertical centre, crease, and unfold.

3. Fold the upper edges to the same crease, but only crease where shown.

4. Make a crease that starts where the last two creases meet and goes out to just short of the outer corners.

5. Put all the creases in together, forming an inside reverse fold.

6. If you're lucky, the paper will look like this. If not, unfold and try again! Repeat steps 2 to 5 on the right-hand side.

7. Fold the upper left flap down and right.

8. Carefully ease out the top wing to the dotted position, then flatten the paper so it stays in shape.

9. Swing the wings over to the left.

10. This is the result. Repeat steps 7 to 9 on the other side.

11. This should be the state of play so far. Turn the paper over.

12. Fold the side of the body to the centre, squashing the paper flat at the base of the wings. The exact position of the squash isn't vital, but try to match the drawings. Repeat on the other side.

13. This should be the result. Turn the paper over.

14. Squash the body to a narrow point.

15. Focus on the head now.

16. Make an inside reverse fold (the paper stays 3D).

17. Turn the paper over. Fold, squash, or otherwise bodge the point of the reversed corner to one side to lock it into position.

18. Turn the paper over for the completed wee beastie.

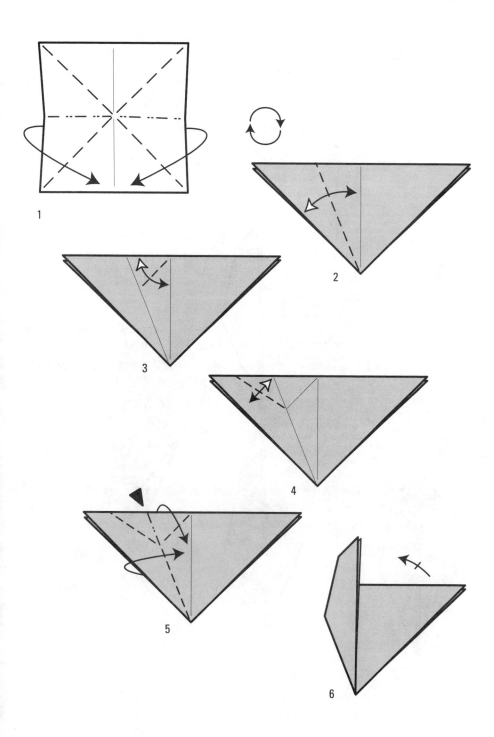

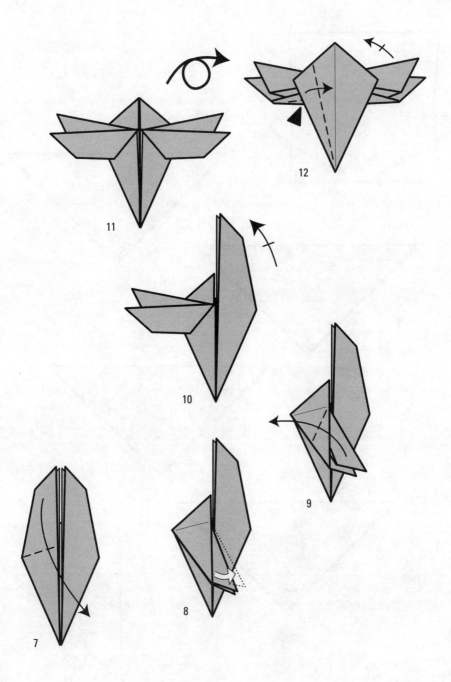

7

8

9

10

11

12

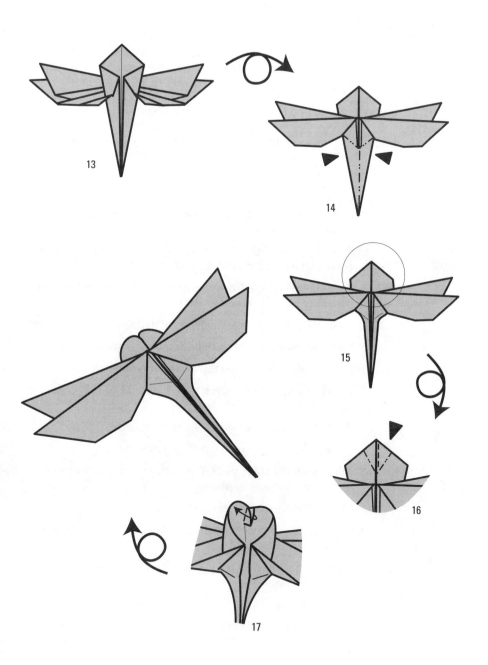

Snail

For many years Robert Lang has been at the forefront of origami in both artistic and technical terms. As well as his own superb creations, he's developed software to help people create their own designs, which you can read all about in Chapter 10.

Unusually, this model makes use of 60-degree geometry to form the basic shape. This produces a narrower form than would be possible from a kite base.

1. Start with a square, white side up, with a diagonal creased. Fold the upper and left corners together, adding a light reference crease.

2. Fold the ends of the diagonals together and add just the ends of the other diagonal.

3. Fold starting at the lower corner, so that the right corner lies on the crease made in step 1.

4. Fold the coloured edge back to the right-hand folded edge.

5. Fold the left edge to the right edge.

6. Fold back to the left, so the paper is symmetrical.

7. Fold the short white edges to the vertical centre, creasing as far as the existing crease.

8. Fold the long raw white edges to the centre.

9. This is the result. Focus on the circled area.

10. Make a small rabbit's ear. The valley crease is new; the others are already in place.

11. This is the result. Repeat on the right.

12. Fold the upper section behind, allowing the rabbit's ear flaps to swing upwards.

13. Fold the narrow flap to the left so that the edge lies on the circled corner.

14. This is the result. Turn the paper over.

15. Fold the main part of the model in half to the left, forming a slender rabbit's ear in the process. Check the next drawing for guidance.

16. Carefully ease out the layers from within the narrow flap.

17. Fold the flap in half, revealing the white side. Repeat on the underside. This move is known in the trade as a *colour change*.

18. Open out the main part of the model.

19. Fold the coloured edges to the vertical centre on both sides.

20. Fold the edges in again. The exact location isn't critical.

21. Fold the model in half from right to left.

22. Rotate the paper to this position. Now focus on the left end.

23. Fold the left corner to the lower corner.

24. Fold the lower left edge to the vertical edge, creasing through all layers. Unfold again.

25. Make a rabbit's ear on the upper layer.

26. Repeat step 25 on the lower flap.

27. Swing the narrow point behind and down to match the next drawing.

28. Repeat the step 27.

29. Repeat again, as many times as you can manage!

30. Make a gentle squash between the eye-stalks to make the head3D.

31. Your snail is ready to crawl!

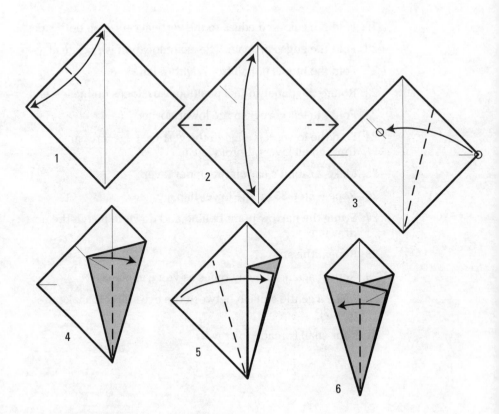

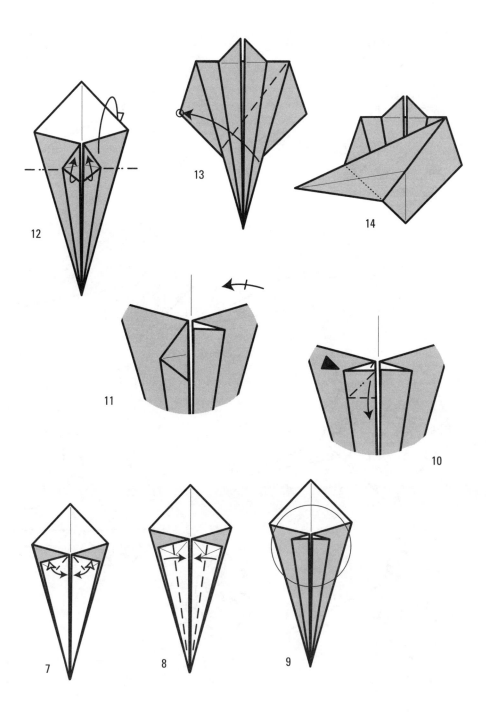

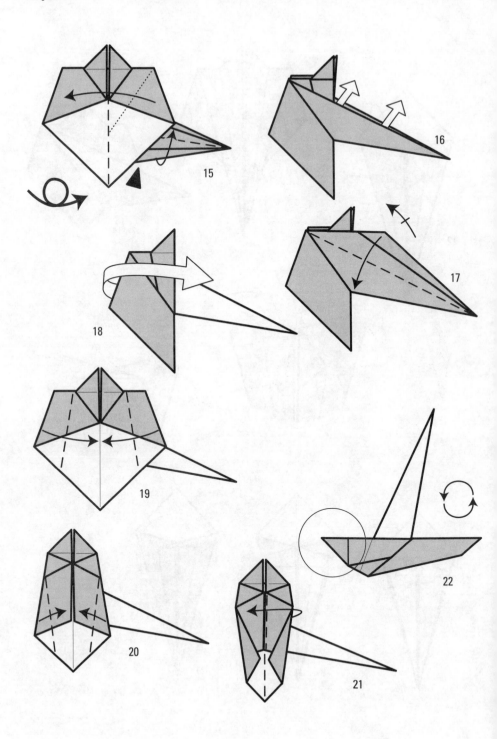

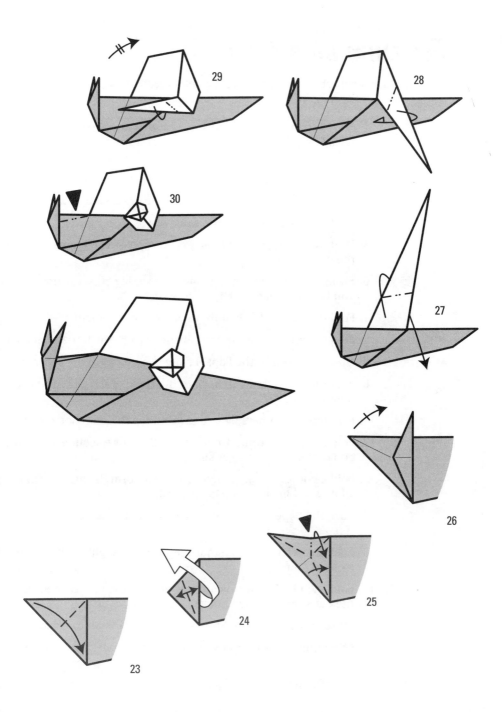

For Dummies Man

As an example of how you might meet a creative challenge, I include an origami version of the *For Dummies* character.

1. Start with a square, white side upwards, and crease both diagonals. Fold the lower corner to the centre and the top corner behind to the centre.

2. Leave a small gap, then fold the corner back down again.

3. Fold the upper edges to the vertical centre, crease, and unfold.

4. Fold the lower edges in the same way.

5. Fold over using the original diagonal, passing the crease through the upper layers.

6. Swing the corners down, using the existing creases shown. (Here you have a variation of the fish base.)

7. Fold the central flaps both ways for reinforcement.

8. Fold the lower edges of the central flaps to the horizontal crease

9. Open and squash the flaps, laying one on top of the other.

10. Fold the end of the flap back to the right, and repeat on the layer underneath.

11. Fold the two corners behind to lie on the (hidden) horizontal edge.

12. Fold the lower corner to the top of the white section. Fold either end of the top edge over slightly.

13. Fold a corner behind a hidden edge to form the mouth. Fold the white section at the top downwards.

14. Turn the paper over. Fold a small section back upwards at the top.

15. Fold the two corners so that they overlap slightly. These form the locks of hair.

16. Fold each half of the lower edge to meet the vertical centre. Tuck the curls into a handy pocket.

17. Make firm creases from the top corners to the bottom centre.

18. Open these creases to half way to form a base. Turn the paper over.

19. Your Dummies man is complete.

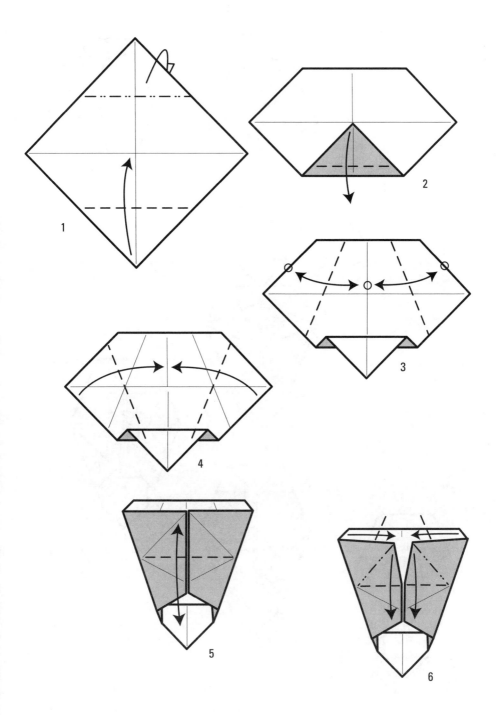

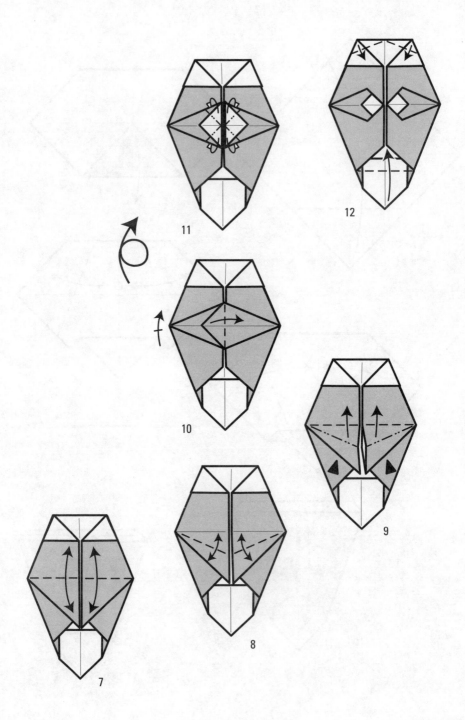

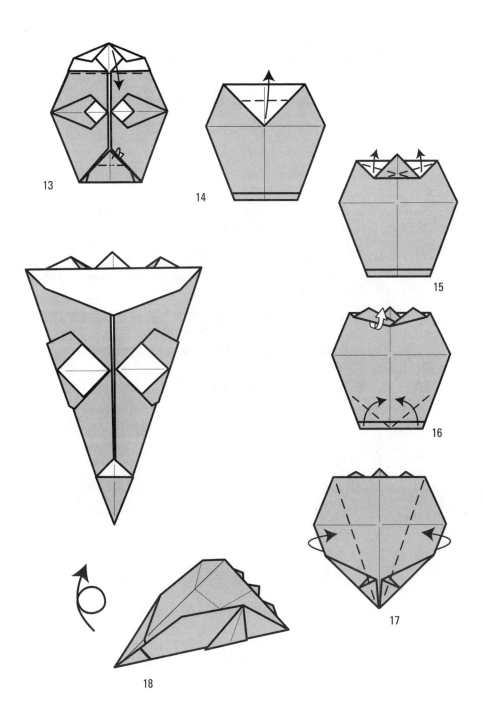

Mystery Object Solution

In case you've not spotted it, the design in question is a humane spider trap. Spiders are wonderful creatures that do much to make our life mo⟨re⟩ pleasant, even if you wouldn't want to find one on your pillow at night. Anything you can do to preserve their tiny lives is vital. Here's how the trap operates:

1. You notice a spider loose in your bedroom. Quickly fold a spide⟨r⟩ trap of suitable size and cock it.

2. Remembering to approach from downwind, slowly and quietly stalk your prey.

3. Release the device to produce just enough weight to stun the creature (use of paper heavier than 140 gsm may result in perm⟨a⟩nent injury to the arachnid. Neither author nor publisher will accept any liability for this).

4. Quickly scoop the dazed spider into the waiting pocket and allo⟨w⟩ it to close, thus preventing escape.

5. Release your captive into a carefully prepared living environment.

6. Feel good about yourself.

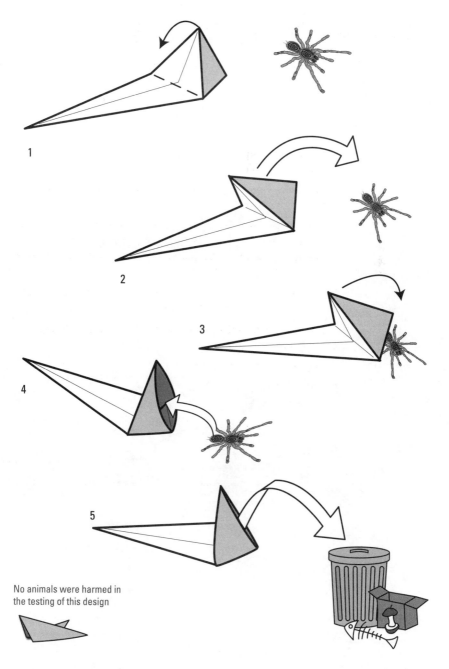

1

2

3

4

5

No animals were harmed in
the testing of this design

Droodle Solution

The Droodle model is, of course, a witch who has fallen off a ship!

Chapter 6

Puzzling Over Geometric Models

In This Chapter

▶ Stars, stripes, and emblems

▶ A biscuit bowl for an aged cat

▶ A house to blow down

*A*ll origami relies on geometry to some extent, but the designs in this chapter use it explicitly in the final form. Geometric modular designs produce extraordinarily beautiful results, especially if you select your colour combinations carefully.

Modular designs are, in essence, geometric shapes that have flaps and pockets that can tuck into each other. The best designs have strong 'locks' so the final design holds together well. Others require a more delicate touch! Some modulars are three-dimensional, others are flat.

In this chapter I cover a wide variety of models, from house bricks and cat bowls to stars and polyhedra (a many-sided shape). You need to fold *even more* accurately than usual to get the best results with these designs!

Modular Star

The keys to a successful star are that the folding sequence uses precise location points and that the units lock firmly into each other. The typical configuration of a modular unit includes a flap and a pocket for the flap to slide into. In some cases good old friction is all that keeps things from falling apart, but my design has an extra lock to hold the units together.

Tiny modular designs look truly exquisite, but have a go at the basic assembly with larger squares before attempting to go miniature! Choose crisp and highly decorative paper.

As with many modular models, the final unit is usually the hardest to fit and lock into place. You need to be careful not to tear the layer you're getting into. Gently pressing the folded spine of the star's point will open the layers nicely.

1. Start with a square, white side upwards. Fold a kite base (Chapter 3 shows you how).

2. Fold the upper triangular flap down over the layers.

3. Unfold the side flaps.

4. Fold the lower corner to the other circled corner, creasing only in the left half of the paper.

5. Repeat the step on the opposite side.

6. Mountain fold the left half of the paper behind.

7. This is the result. Rotate the paper 180 degrees. To keep you on your toes, I ask you to turn the paper over from top to bottom!

8. Fold the small corner flap over the folded edge, crease firmly, and unfold.

9. Unfold the upper flap.

10. Make an outside reverse fold, wrapping the layers around to the left.

11. This is the complete unit. Look carefully at what goes into what!

12. Arrange two units as shown and slide the upper one into the lower one, so that the circled points meet.

13. Carefully ease your finger (or some other small object) in between the layers and refold the flap you creased in step 8. Continue in the same way with the other units to complete the star.

14. Adding these creases enables you to try for a five-pointed star if you're feeling adventurous.

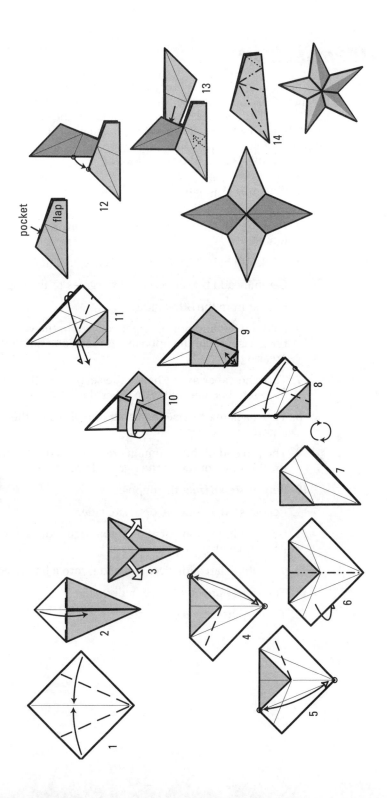

Hexahedron

This design dates from my very early days of creating origami, in the mid 1980s. Several other designs produced an identical shape, but they all had creases or edges that spoiled the shape of the finished design. I wanted the faces to be unsullied. This model requires a delicate touch in handling the paper during the later stages, but this is no bad trait to develop.

1. Start with a square, coloured side up. Book-fold it in half and unfold. Turn the paper over.

2. Fold the left and right edges to the centre, crease, and unfold.

3. Book-fold in half horizontally, crease, and unfold.

4. Carefully add two creases at 45 degrees to the edges.

5. Repeat from the other side.

6. Fold top left and bottom right corners to the vertical quarter creases. Fold the opposite corners, and unfold after creasing.

7. Turn the paper over. Change the sections of the crease shown to become valley on this side.

8. Turn back over. Raise the paper into 3D using the creases shown.

9. The top end of the mountain crease folds over to the furthest inside corner, as the right side rises up.

10. Repeat step 8 from the opposite side.

11. Repeat step 9 from the opposite side.

12. Gently fold the top left and bottom right corners together, using the valley diagonal crease.

13. The white flap folds over and slides into a handy pocket.

14. The same happens on the underside.

15. The hexahedron is complete.

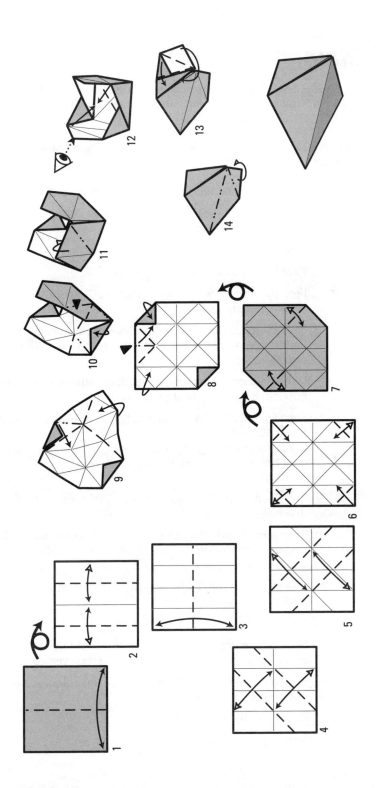

Emblem

Edwin Corrie's Emblem is a pleasing geometric design that arose from a familiar starting point, the bird base, but the design doesn't betray its origins too obviously.

Edwin Corrie is noted for his animals and birds, all of which have a geometric feel to them.

1. Pre-crease and collapse into a preliminary base.

2. Pre-crease and inside reverse the lower edges to form the bird base.

3. Fold the first lower corner to the top.

4. Fold the lower left section upwards.

5. Fold the narrow flaps over to meet the horizontal centre, crease, and unfold.

6. Fold the same flaps back along their own outer edges, starting the crease where the previous crease meets the vertical centre.

7. Unfold a layer from deep, deep, deep within. You're undoing one of the folds in step 2.

8. Start to fold along the creases shown. The valley crease facing the 'press here' arrow also needs to be in place on the layer of paper immediately underneath, exposed as the paper opens. The next drawing is seen from the viewpoint of the eye.

9. The open 3D flap now re-flattens outwards (check the next drawing).

10. This is the result. It's not so bad once you see what's happening, is it? Rotate the paper 180 degrees and repeat steps 7 to 9 on the matching side.

11. Making a new valley crease, swivel the mountain crease so it lies on the vertical centre.

12. Like this, repeat on the other side.

13. Starting the crease at the right corner, fold the lower corner so it lies on the circled area of the crease.

14. Ease out some white paper and tuck the coloured section underneath it.

15. Repeat on the other end.

16. Rotate to this position. Neat isn't it?

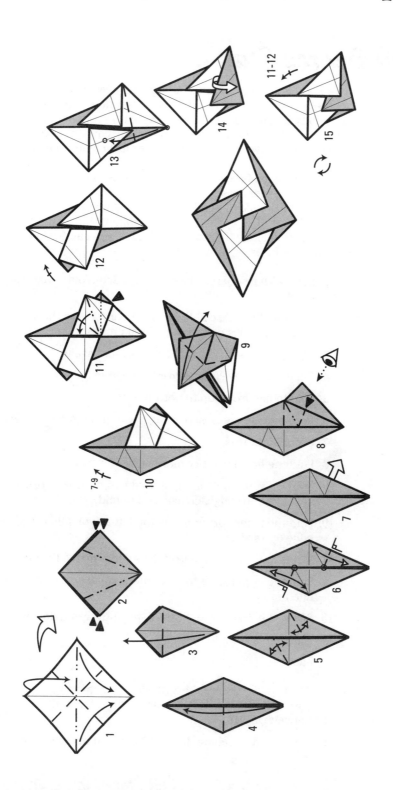

60-Degree Star

David Petty is a highly creative folder who specialises in rings, wreaths, and modular designs. He loves to explore variations that produce subtly different patterns. This star has many variations – play around with the design and see if you can discover your own variations! Being creative is fun and you might just create something new

The essential geometry of this design is based around a 60-degree angle, which in most cases, produces six-pointed stars. However, if you make five units and bend the paper slightly, you can often create a 3D star of some kind with five points. Similarly, by making a mountain fold along the axis of each unit, you can try joining more than six units.

1. Start with a square, white side up. Book-fold in half and unfold.

2. Starting the crease at the top left corner, fold the lower corner so it lies on the horizontal crease.

3. The model looks like this so far. Unfold again.

4. Repeat the move as a mirror image from the top right corner.

5. Fold in half from top to bottom.

6. Refold these creases, passing them through both layers.

7. Unfold upwards.

8. Fold the bottom left corner over.

9. Starting at the bottom right, fold the lower left corner back along the raw edge, crease, and unfold.

10. Fold the inner corner to the top left as you fold the lower edge upwards.

11. Inside reverse the lower right corner to match the other side.

12. Fold the upper edge to meet the vertical crease, crease, and unfold.

13. Swing the first corner at the top left over and down.

14. The unit is complete.

Assembly

1. Arrange two units as shown, sliding them so that the circled corners coincide. The top flap of the lower unit slides between layers.

2. Fold this flap behind, locking the two units together.

3. Slide in the third unit in a similar fashion. Repeat with the other three units.

4. Carefully fold behind the six flaps as shown.

5. The star complete from this side.

6. Turn the paper over to see the star from the other side.

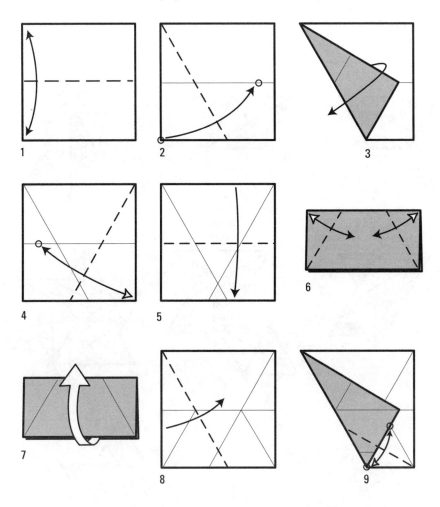

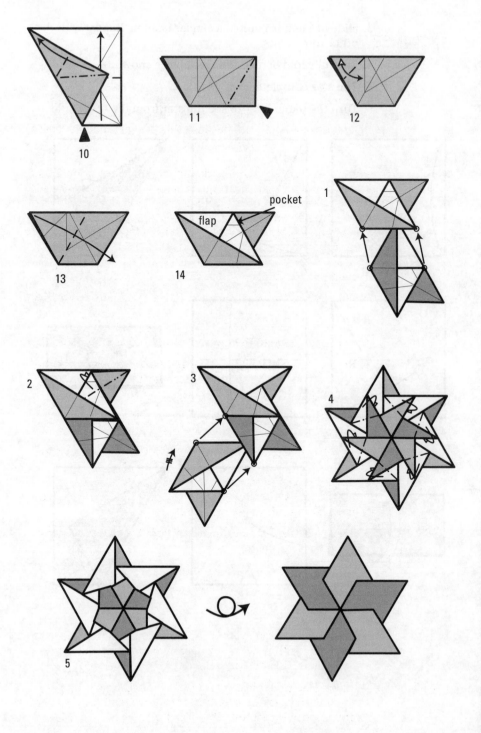

Gomez Bowl

Here's a design that'll appeal to lovers of pre-creasing; people who like to put in all the major creases first and then assemble the model. Gomez is my ageing cat, now 21, stone deaf, and looking a bit threadbare. He mentioned in passing that it was about time I named a model after him and because this design functions well as a feeding bowl, this was his big chance.

The model may look like hard work, but in actual fact, adding the creases one at a time to an open square is probably the easiest way to ensure neatness and accuracy, as long as you check carefully each time to identify the location for the crease. As with most origami models, your first effort may look a little scruffy (mine always do!) but by the third version, you'll be able to give the model some finesse!

1. Start with a square, white side up. Add both diagonals.

2. Fold each corner to the centre, crease, and unfold (blintzing).

3. Fold each edge to the centre, crease, and unfold.

4. Fold each edge to the quarter crease, crease, and unfold.

5. Rotate the paper 45 degrees. Fold the lower corner to the opposite intersection of the diagonal and blintz, creasing the outer sections only and unfold.

6. Rotate again. Fold the lower edge to the opposite quarter crease, again creasing only the outer sections.

7. This is another small pre-crease. Look at the two location points. The lower corner will lie on the diagonal, the circled points on the right will coincide as well, but you only crease the small valley in the centre. Make sure you understand this *before* you do it!

8. This is the crease pattern so far. Turn the paper over and focus on a corner section.

9. Add a valley crease where shown.

10. Add another.

11. Add yet another!

12. Add two more valley pre-creases. You can make these both at the same time. Repeat three times, rotating the paper each time. Turn the paper over.

    At long last, the creasing is complete and we can start to fold the thing. From here onwards, you won't need to add any more creases. Not intentionally, anyway!

13. Collapse one corner using the creases shown.

14. Fold the central section down.

15. Inside reverse the two upper corners.

16. Fold the corner underneath. The eye shows the angle you look at next.

17. Turn the paper over. Tuck the flap into the pocket, trapping the reversed corners.

18. The corner is complete. Zooming out and turning the paper over, you see the finished corner. All you now need to do is to repeat steps 13 to 18 on the three other corners!

19. This is the result. Fold the bowl into 3D as shown.

20. Complete? Congratulations!

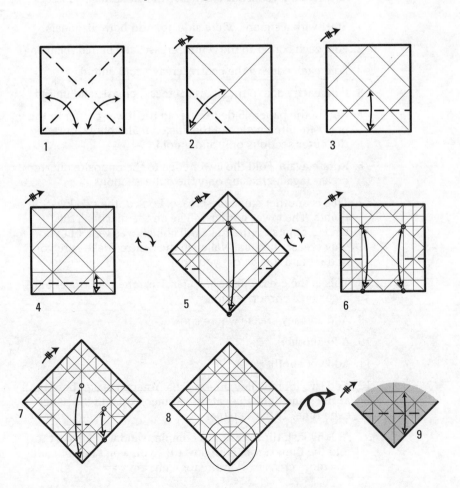

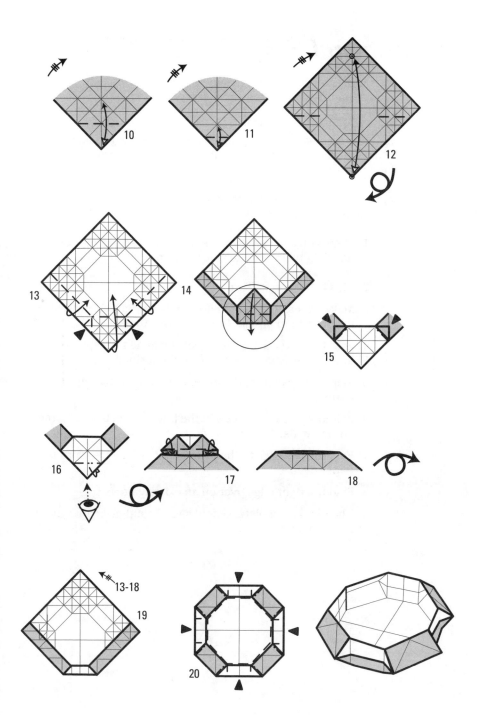

Pentagonal Star

Dave Brill is one of those rare folders who can seemingly turn his hand to any style of folding and still create classics. He is deeply interested in the underlying geometry of paper and has produced many modular designs. This is one of his simpler designs, producing a five-pointed star. The geometry doesn't quite produce perfect 72-degree angles, so the end result is a star that doesn't quite lie flat, but it's close enough!

Stars are endlessly popular in origami and make perfect gifts as Christmas tree decorations.

1. Start with a square, white side up, creased along a diagonal. Fold two opposite sides to lie on the diagonal.

2. This is the result. Turn the paper over.

3. Make a crease from top left to bottom right corners, allowing the flap to flip out from underneath.

4. Fold the lower left corner over the folded edge, and the lower right underneath in a similar fashion.

5. Make a crease from the lower mid-point to the top right corner.

6. Fold the upper raw edge to the lower edge, bisecting the corner angle.

7. Fold the left edge to the nearest coloured edge. Turn the paper over.

8. Fold the right edge over on an existing crease.

9. The unit is complete. Unfold slightly and make four more identical units.

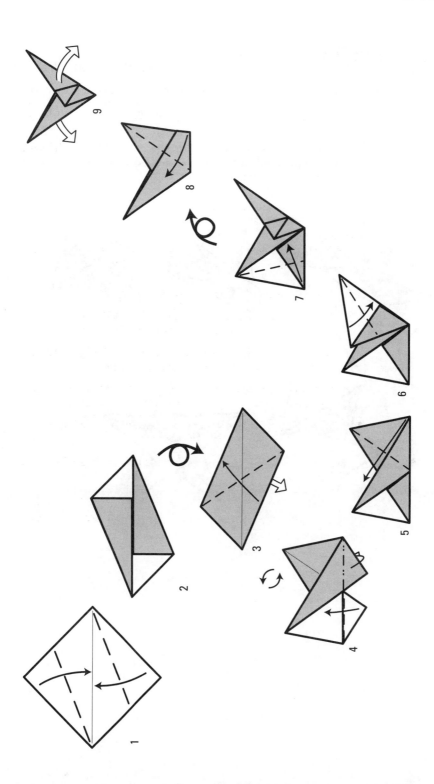

Assembly

1. Arrange one unit over another so that the circled points meet.

2. Fold the white section over, partially tucking it into a pocket.

3. Fold the matching flap behind in the same way (or turn over and repeat).

4. The two units are joined. Add the other three in the same way. The paper will have slight tension.

5. Your star is ready to shine.

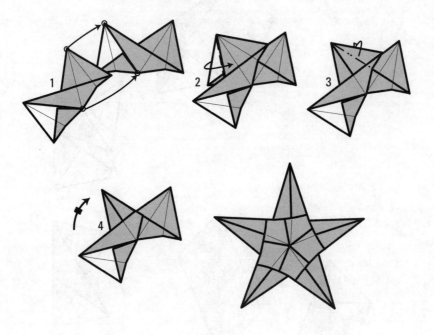

Fluted Module

Cubes are endlessly fascinating to origami designers, probably because the concept is so simple that anyone can grapple with it while creating. I even know of a folder who makes units while driving to work every day, but I can't recommend that approach if you want a long and happy life! Rocky Jardes' design has loose flaps that give a pleasingly organic feel to the finished cube.

As with all modular designs, you need to fold very neatly and accurately so that all the units are *exactly* the same as each other. Folding with crisp paper helps the final model to keep its intended shape.

1. Start with a square, coloured side up. Book-fold in half horizontally and unfold.

2. Make a light pinch to mark the lower mid-point.

3. Fold the upper and lower edges to the centre.

4. Using the pinch mark as reference, fold all four corners out as far as they'll go (without tearing), starting from the centre of the paper.

5. Unfold the two sections.

6. Fold the outer edges to opposite horizontal creases, and then unfold.

7. Turn the paper over. Refold the horizontal creases through the extra flaps.

8. Repeat step 6 on this side.

9. Turn the paper over. Convert the creases to valleys only where shown.

10. Form the paper into 3D, taking the lower left corner to the circled point.

11. Repeat the move on the other side.

Bringing down the house

Origami Australia built an origami house big enough to walk into, complete with origami furniture and decorations. They used over one square kilometre of paper and over 15,000 separate creases resulting in 395 bricks. Over 2,000 man hours were needed and 4,512 cups of coffee! You can find photos at www.papercrane.org/index/Projects/78.

Rotate the paper so you see the move from the same perspective.

12. Fold over the outer corners and crease firmly so they're at 90 degrees to the central section. Fold six such units.

13. Arrange two as shown and slide the left unit over the right so the corner flap meets the inner corner on the right.

14. Interlock the third unit, tucking corners into pockets. (You need three hands to do this easily.)

15. Repeat the folds on the underside, tucking all six units neatly into each other.

16. Congratulate yourself and have a cup of tea!

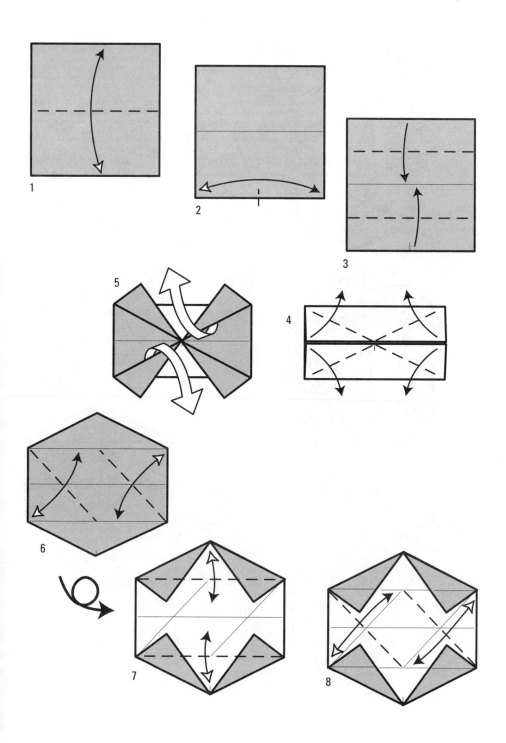

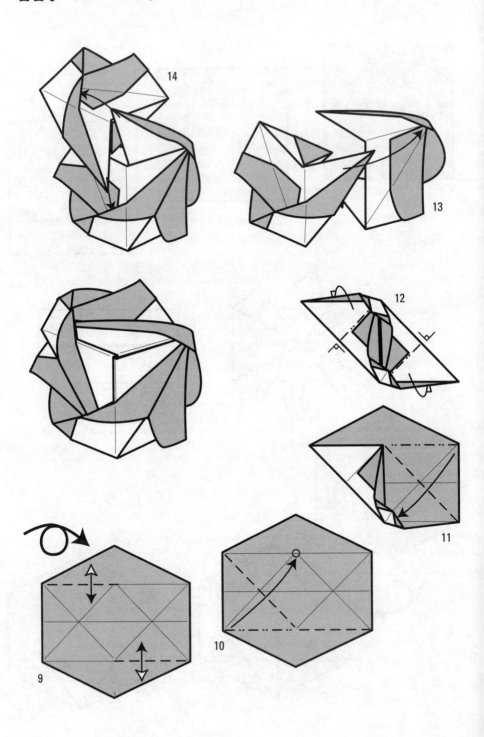

House

You might think that the shape of a typical house wouldn't present a huge problem in origami design. However, when you start to look into it, you realise it requires some thought, especially if you want the external face of the house to be 'clean', with no extra creases or folded edges visible. Here's a solution by Wayne Brown, a modest and little-known origami creator, who's been one of my closest origami friends and collaborators for over 25 years. The folding sequence is of my own devising.

The paper here is of A4 proportions, but you can fold this design from most rectangles, simply resulting in wider or narrower houses.

1. Start with a rectangle, white side upwards, creased in half. Fold the upper and lower edges to the centre, crease, and unfold.

2. Fold a short edge to a long edge, starting at the corner. Crease only as far as the central crease. Repeat on all corners.

3. Make vertical creases that pass *exactly* through the intersections of the creases.

4. Turn the paper over. Pinch the mountain crease and fold it over to the vertical crease, flattening to create the valley crease. (This is a little unusual, but the easiest method.) Repeat on all corners.

5. Here's an enlarged view of the circled area. Fold the circled points to meet, creasing only where shown.

6. Fold the lower quarter behind.

7. Make the short crease through both layers and unfold.

8. Turn the paper over. Carefully identify the circled location and add a valley crease from it to the edge.

9. Fold the vertical edge to the horizontal edge as far as you can on the existing crease.

10. Take the folded edge to the second vertical crease, then unfold fully.

11. Fold the corner to the circled location, creasing only where shown.

12. Make a pleat, allowing the paper to rise up as it wants.

13. Make the valley crease through the top two layers, then unfold fully.

14. You should have these creases (and hopefully no others!). Repeat steps 5 to 13 on the remaining three corners.

15. Rotate the paper 90 degrees. Make the valley crease shown at both ends.

16. Turn the paper over. Form one end of the house into 3D using pleats.

17. Refold the creases made in step 13.

18. Refold the creases made in step 10.

19. Tuck in the bottom of the house.

20. Repeat steps 16 to 19 at the other end.

21. Your house is ready to move into.

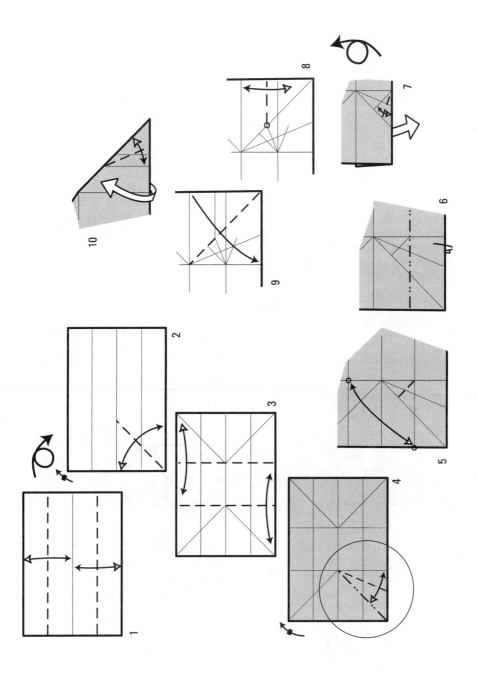

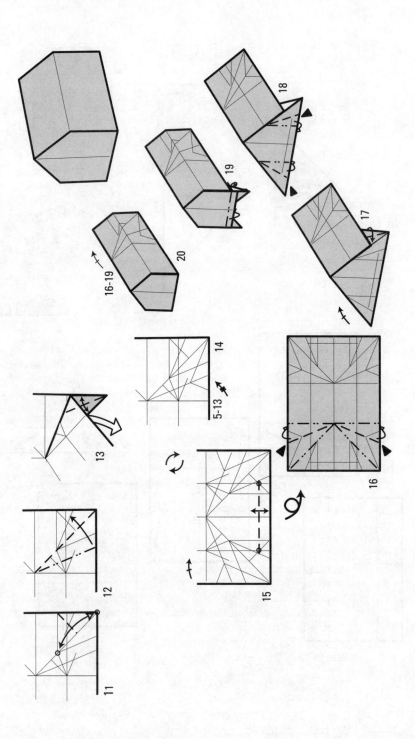

Chapter 7

Facing the Challenging Models

* *

In This Chapter

▶ Frogs, dogs, and dragons

▶ Decorative twists and boxes

▶ A touch of Christmas

* *

*T*he series of designs in this chapter are intended to test your skills. Experienced folders might not consider some of the models to be a real challenge, but these things are relative. If you really want to try your hand at complex work, check out the website of the Tanteidan (detectives) who specialise in advanced work (www. origami.gr.jp/index0.html). Their bi-monthly magazine contains a lot of complex folding!

Where a base is required, I've assumed you can fold to that starting point (refer to Chapter 3 if you need more info on bases).

Start with a larger square than usual, which helps you with subtler steps.

Don't assume you'll finish the complex models the first time – you may need to abandon one halfway through and refold from scratch. The second attempt will be cleaner and may get you over the hurdle. If not, do the best you can and lay the model aside for a few days. Your mind often considers and resolves problems when you're not concentrating on them – and this also applies to origami. Many creative folders have a sheet of paper by their bedside in case they wake up with a bright idea!

Try to make each model at least three times and compare the first with the last – you should notice a marked improvement in the finesse. This is because you've overcome the difficulty of following the instructions and can focus on making edges meet perfectly and creating sharp, accurate creases.

Chinese Frog

Roman Diaz is a folder from Uruguay, and one of the rising stars of
origami. His designs show a mastery of technique, character, and
elegance. He makes highly complex designs, but luckily also
delights in simpler folds! In this model he starts with a traditional
Chinese design, which he then adapts and extends as his creative
instinct takes over.

1. Start with a square, creased with the Union Jack pattern
   (refer to the waterbomb base in Chapter 3). Fold all four
   corners to the centre.

2. Turn the paper over and fold the two upper corners to the
   centre.

3. Fold the two lower corners to the centre, but crease only
   the upper half of the possible crease. Unfold the flaps.

4. Turn the paper over. Fold the inner corner to the lower
   edge, crease, and unfold.

5. Fold the upper flap in half upwards.

6. Fold both sides to the vertical centre.

7. Open the lower corners out, folding on the (dotted) valley
   crease.

8. This is the result. Turn the paper over.

9. Open the pockets slightly to suggest eyes.

10. Make a slight mountain crease to shape the body, and ease
    down the lower jaw. This is the traditional Chinese sitting
    frog.

11. Make two mountain creases to fold the back legs, er,
    backwards.

12. This is the traditional Chinese *jumping* frog!

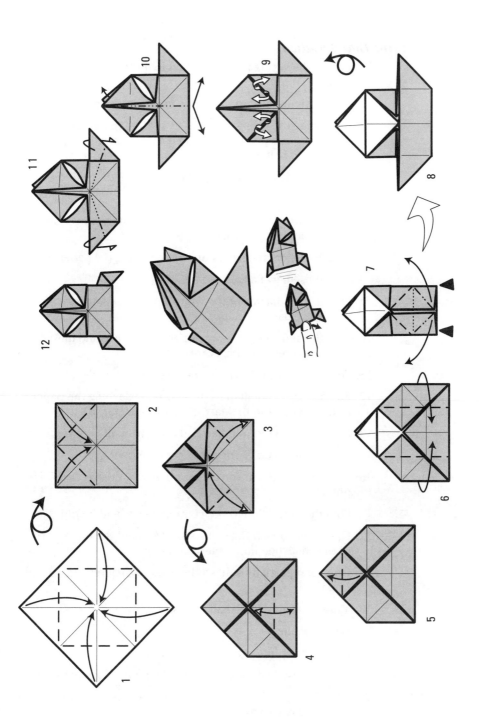

The Diaz Variation

1. Unfold the sitting frog. Mountain fold the upper and lower corners.

2. Fold both upper corners to the centre of the paper.

3. Rearrange the layers of paper by folding the lower white corners to the centre as you fold the small white square sections in half upwards.

4. Fold the sides underneath, allowing two flaps to fold out.

5. This is the result. Turn the paper over.

6. Fold the top flap in half, open and squash the lower section as you did in step 7 earlier.

7. Ease two hidden corners upwards, pulling the paper out.

8. Fold these new flaps down.

9. Fold the top halves of the white square sections in half, flattening the paper beneath.

10. Fold the short edge to the horizontal, crease and unfold (A); inside reverse this corner (B).

11. Fold these two corners over – check the next drawing.

12. Fold the tip of the flap to the centre, squashing the paper to do so (A). Fold the narrowed leg back out (B).

13. Ease out the coloured flap and tuck the white areas into it.

14. This is the result. Turn the paper over.

15. Fold the corners at the centre outwards, crease, and unfold.

16. Fold the 'nose' flap to the centre, crease, and unfold.

17. Open and squash the eye socket (A). Fold the outer corner of the squashed flap underneath (B).

18. Open and partially squash the eyes so they remain 3D and froggy.

19. Make a crimp through all layers.

20. Unfold again.

21. Ease out the hidden layer at the bottom.

22. Form the body into 3D, keeping the point of the back out.

23. Fold the paper back underneath to lock the fold in place. Open the jaw slightly.

24. Your little amphibian is complete.

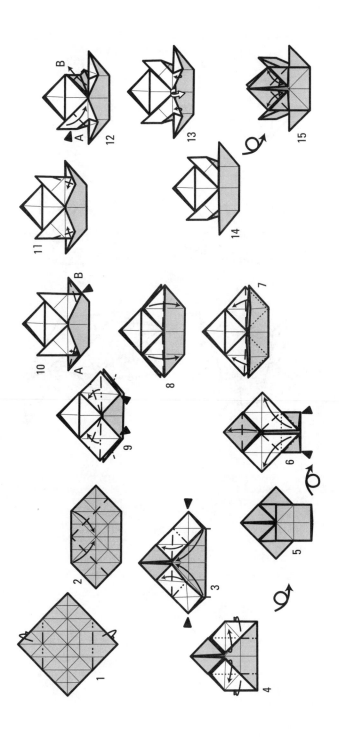

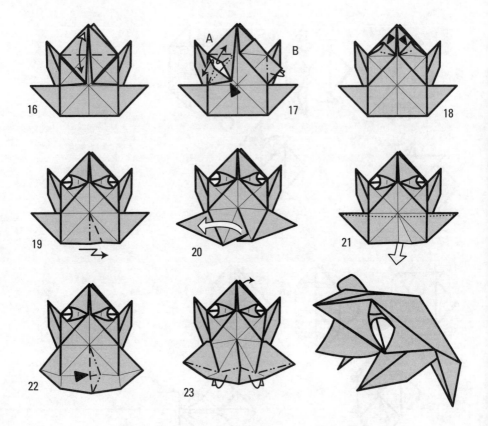

Dragon

Eric Joisel is world-renowned for his expressive and artistic paper sculptures, but he's also a master of the classic bases. He uses the slightly obscure blintzed fish base in this model.

A blintz base reduces the working area by half, so use a larger square.

This model has a number of subtle techniques, such as the crimp in step 19 and the formation of the nose in step 20 – persevere with these to feel more in control of them. You can practise techniques like these by using a separate sheet and only folding the relevant area of the model; for example, you could practise step 15 on a kite base.

Try folding a blintzed kite base and see if you can design anything new – many wonderful new creations are discovered by adapting existing designs. (Remember to credit your inspiration if you produce diagrams.)

1. Start with a square, white side up. Book-fold in half both ways.
2. Blintz all corners and turn the paper over.
3. Fold both left edges to the horizontal centre, allowing flaps to flip from behind.
4. Inside reverse the flaps on the right, again allowing flaps to flip from behind.
5. This is known as a blintzed fish base.
6. Turn the paper over and crease two diagonals.
7. Collapse the sides down (as you would with a preliminary base).
8. Swing the upper flap on the right over to the left, repeating underneath. A minor miracle!
9. Petal fold the top flap (as you would with a bird base).
10. Repeat underneath.
11. Swap the flaps over again.
12. Fold the white corners over, then tuck underneath the first layer. Repeat behind.
13. Inside reverse the upper left flap to the dotted position.
14. Inside reverse the tail, but to a more tail-like angle.
15. Outside reverse the head downwards.

16. Narrow the tail by folding the upper edges inside as far as you can. The fold extends to the end of the dotted line.

17. This is the result. Time to focus on the head.

18. Make a double reverse fold to form the snout of the beast.

19. Hold the head firmly and make an outside crimp on both sides.

20. Fold the nose over to taste.

21. Stand well back in case you get scorched . . .

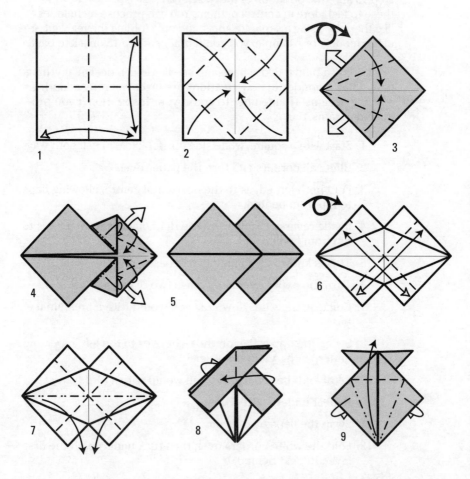

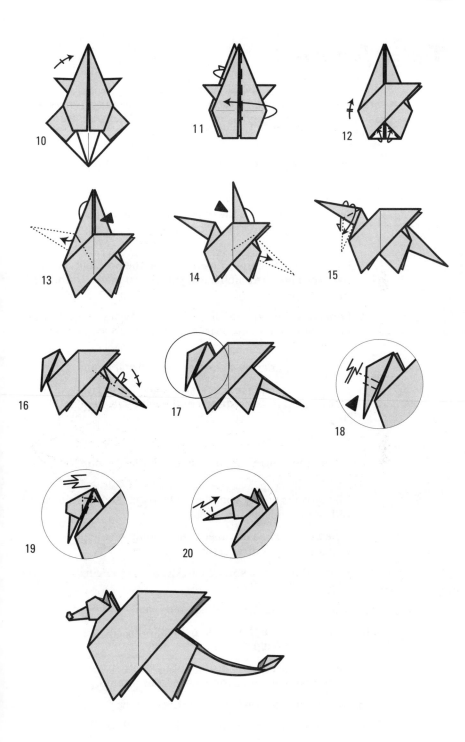

Twist Flower

Yoshihide Momotani is one of Japan's origami masters. For over 40 years he's maintained an extraordinary creative output, encompassing many different styles and techniques. The twist used here is an elegant and creatively useful technique.

1. Form a waterbomb base with the colour outside (refer to Chapter 3).

2. Starting at the centre of the lower edge, fold the first corner on the right over so the edge lies at right angles to the vertical. Make a gentle pinch to mark the upper edge of the crease.

3. Fold the upper corner down, making the horizontal crease pass through the pinch mark you've just made. Unfold back to the square.

4. Looking at the square formed by the creases in the centre, refold any mountain creases so that the creases are all valleys.

5. Rotate the paper by 45 degrees and turn it over.

6. Make a valley crease that starts at the lower corner of the central square and extends to the left edge. Repeat three more times.

7. Partially form these creases so the paper becomes 3D.

8. Rotate the central square anti-clockwise, folding the paper on the valley creases.

9. The move is nearly complete. The paper should fold naturally and needs no new creases.

10. When the twist is complete, this should be the position. Reinforce the central creases as valleys.

11. Rotate the central square clockwise, rearranging the flaps underneath it.

12. This is the result. Turn the paper over.

13. Fold each white triangle in half, allowing the paper to open up into a round petal form.

14. Carefully turn a petal inside out by gently pressing from underneath while wrapping the sides around.

15. Repeat the step on the other three petals.

16. Turn the paper over for the completed flower.

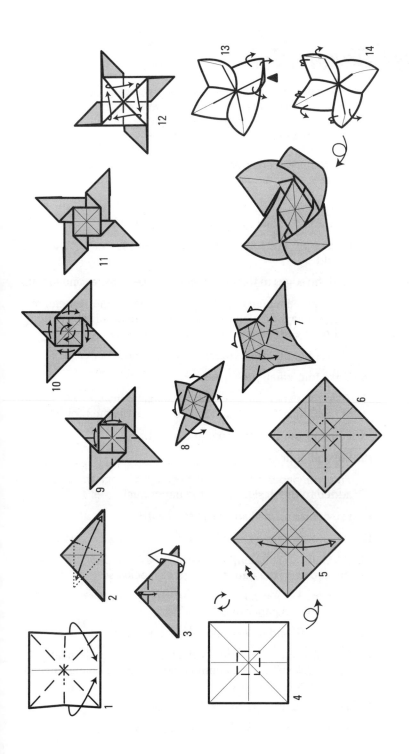

Twist Decoration

Although he gave up actively folding many years ago, Jeff Beynon left a huge archive rich in technique, skill, and elegance. Jeff's early work was almost exclusively based on twisting and collapsing the paper towards the centre.

This model requires considerable care when creasing and you may need to make it several times to achieve a clean result.

1. Start with a square, creased on both diagonals, white side upwards. Fold all four corners to the centre.

2. Fold upper and lower edges to the centre, crease, and unfold.

3. Fold the edges to the most recent creases, crease, and unfold.

4. Add the remaining eighth creases as well, being careful to keep the layers in place. Rotate the paper and repeat steps 2–4 on the other axis.

5. This is the creased pattern so far. Turn the paper over.

6. Make four small pre-creases.

7. Turn the paper back over and collapse it inwards like a kind of multi-form base (Chapter 3 describes the multiform base).

8. Fold out the corners from underneath.

9. Pleat all four corners.

10. Turn the paper over to see the colour change the pleats added to the design. Turn the paper back over.

11. Pre-crease a small square in the centre.

12. Do four more pre-creases.

13. Carefully start to emphasise the creases shown, twisting the centre of the paper 90 degrees clockwise.

14. Swing the coloured flaps so that they point the other way and turn the paper over.

15. Pre-crease and reverse the small corners.

16. Fold the flap in half while swivelling a layer underneath at right angles. This is a cunning move that's a lot easier than it sounds.

17. This is the underside. Turn the paper over.

18. The completed decoration. I hope you feel very proud of yourself.

Creative suggestion

You can join several twists together to form a tapestry.

1. Ease out the paper slightly.

2. Tuck the corner of the next unit into the revealed pocket, making sure that the point of the flap goes past the partially unfolded diagonal.

3. Return the layers to their original position. The two should be joined tightly.

4. Repeat for as long as you have patience!

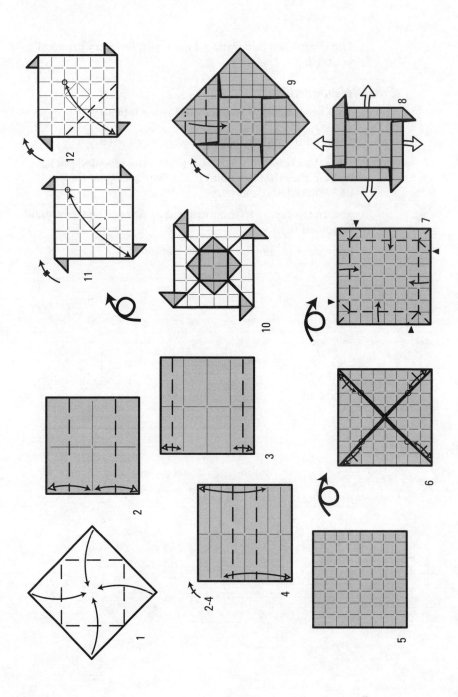

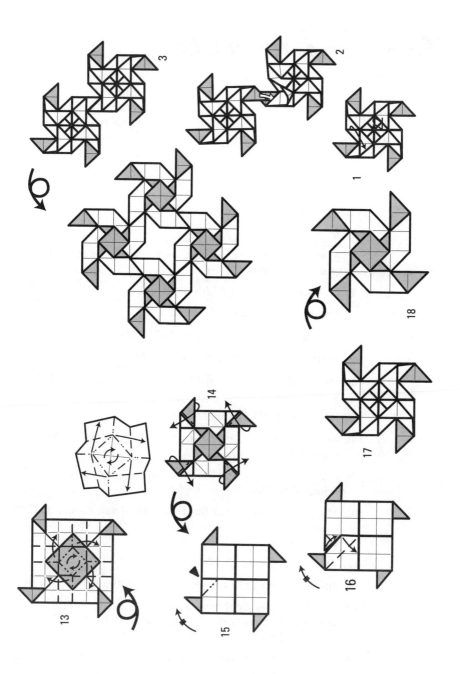

Four-Compartment Box

The late Philip Shen's designs are often containers of some kind and characterised by elegance and tension within the paper. This design isn't one of his easiest creations, but I'm challenging you in this chapter. Once you've mastered the raised central section, the other place you may struggle is in step 18 – be patient and don't force the paper!

When you've made a Shen design you begin to see how his mind worked and appreciate the beauty of his work. You can see his influence in many of my own models.

1. Use the division method I explain in Chapter 3 to identify ⅕ of an edge. Fold the furthest edge from the mark to meet it, crease, and unfold.

2. Add the other central fifth division.

3. Add both diagonals.

4. Add the internal fifth creases on the other axis.

5. Turn the paper over and add both diagonals.

6. Turn back over and collapse the paper into a waterbomb base.

7. Now you need to focus on the top corner.

8. Add two bisectors to the top triangular section. Open the paper fully.

9. Form the paper using the crease shown, creating a small crimped section.

10. The paper should look like this. Unfold and repeat on the three remaining sides. Be patient and try to keep the creases clean!

11. This is the result. Unfold fully.

12. Fold the corners to the crease intersections.

13. Fold the upper right edge to meet the vertical centre crease. Crease only on the white area. Repeat in mirror image and again on the remaining sides.

14. Rotate the paper slightly. Crease through both layers on a crease joining the circled points. Repeat all round.

15. Unfold a corner. Make two small valley creases. Note the two reference points . Refold the corner inwards, unfold another, and repeat all round.

16. Open fully again and reform the central section as in step 9.

17. Fold a corner in on an existing crease.

18. Making a partial reverse fold, start to form the corner using existing creases. Refer to the next drawing (19) for guidance.

19. This is what you're aiming for. Fold the next section over and continue the process all the way round.

20. Gently rotate the dividing flaps anti-clockwise, as you ease open the top point into a twisted square.

21. Complete. Now make the model again more neatly and fill it with sweets!

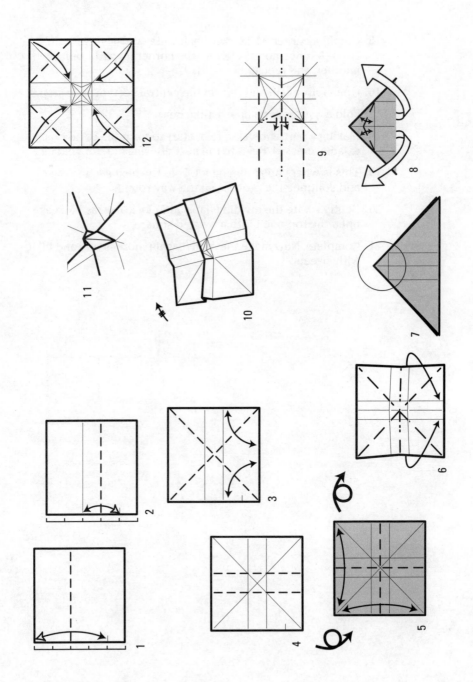

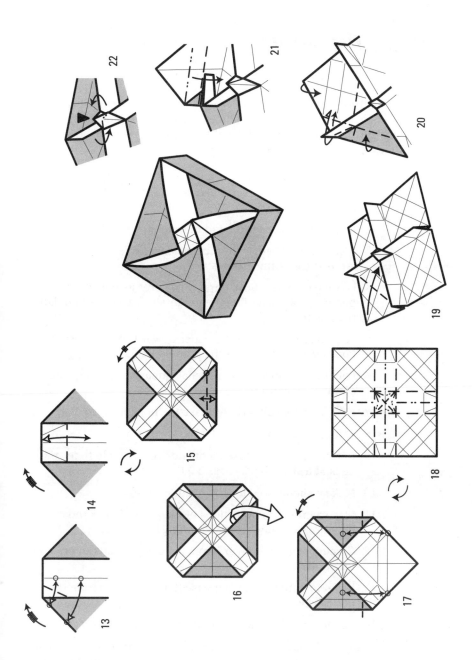

Perro Liberando

Louis Fernandez Perez is a Spaniard with a wicked sense of humour. When this design was first displayed at a British origami convention in the 1980s, a box was placed over it saying 'censored'! Thankfully, we now live in more liberated times and are better able to appreciate the humour. However, if you think the model will offend someone, don't have it on display!

1. Start with a kite base, with the colour outside. Fold the lower edges to the vertical edge, creasing about ⅔ of the way to the centre.

2. Fold the top corner behind to touch the bottom corner.

3. Fold the lower edges to the vertical centre, creasing only as far as the existing creases.

4. Folding on a new horizontal valley crease, collapse the paper upwards, adding the mountain creases as you flatten the paper.

5. Fold the lower half of the paper upwards on a crease that lines up with the top of the pointed flap

6. Fold the tail down, making small squash folds to extend the distance downwards.

7. Fold over a small strip to make the tail appear longer.

8. Fold in half from right to left.

9. Rotate the paper. Make an outside reverse fold to form the neck at a slight backwards angle.

10. Make a similar fold for the head.

11. Make a crimp on both sides of the paper. Check the next diagram carefully before flattening these folds.

12. Carefully ease out layers from inside the head (an origami lobotomy).

13. Reverse both legs, on a crease that follows on from the underlying edge.

14. Reverse the feet back so that the circled points meet.

15. Tuck the back legs underneath layers. Roll over the tip of the head to form a nose (otherwise it would smell bad).

16. Pre-crease and crimp the nose in and out. Shape the front legs.

17. Shape the head, and tuck part of the feet underneath. Now to focus on the rear of the animal!

18. Press in the centre of the tail and adjust the angle down, narrowing it in half. This is a weird kind of sink, but hopefully not too difficult.

19. Reverse the tail upwards at a suitable angle.

The 'complemento'

1. Start with a small strip of suitably coloured paper. Fold both sides to the centre.

2. Make one end pointed, and twist the remainder. Precision isn't necessary here.

3. You can now insert the *complemento* into a small pocket underneath the tail and adjust the angle according to the laws of gravity.

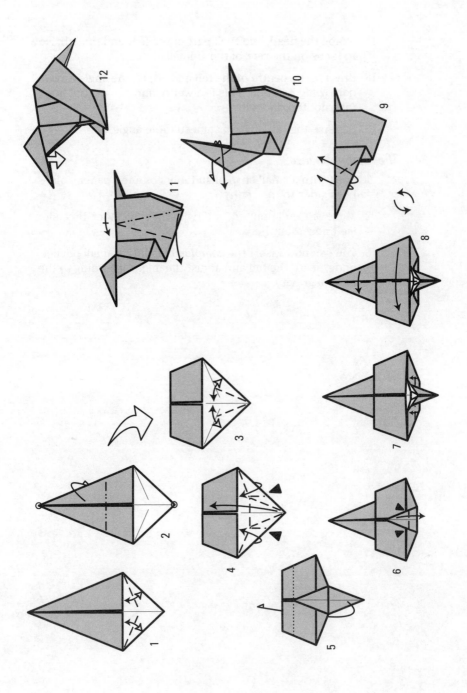

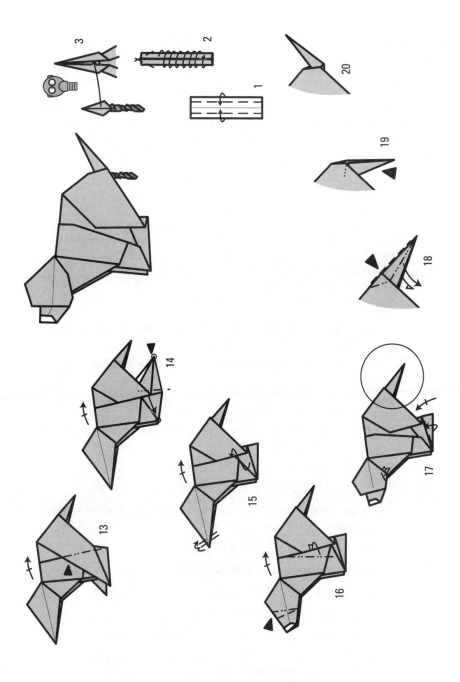

Santa

For over 25 years Ted Norminton has been devising ingenious and unusual designs, yet only a relatively small number have been published. This is a shame, because almost every model he creates incorporates some refreshing or surprising moves. Ted's models are rarely simple to fold; requiring concentration and repeated folding to perfect.

When creating a sequence for a model such as this, you can either pre-crease every move fully, creating a very long sequence that hopefully comes together easily, or you can simply indicate where the creases lie and leave it to the folder to work out how to make them. I've compromised here: the sequence made in steps 29 and 30 is pre-creased right at the start, because it's incredibly difficult for a relative beginner to do neatly without an existing crease. The creases in steps 22–27 *could* be precreased, but these folds are more do-able, so I've left you to do them.

1. Start with an unfolded preliminary base, white side up. Fold in half from bottom to top.

2. Fold the lower right edge to the first crease line.

3. Fold the thicker section underneath.

4. Pull out the first hidden layer from inside.

5. Fold the coloured raw edge to the crease, but only fold the section shown.

6. Fold the new edge to the same crease.

7. Unfold to step 5.

8. Bisect the angle between the raw coloured edge and the nearest crease.

9. Swing the larger flap down and right.

10. Repeat steps 5 to 8 on the matching side.

11. Unfold back to the square.

12. Collapse into a preliminary base.

13. Gently pinch the centre point of the upper layer.

14. Rotate the paper 180 degrees. Fold the lower (closed) corner to the pinch mark, crease, and unfold.

15. Sink the corner.

16. Fold all lower edges to the centre, crease firmly, and unfold.

17. Sink the corners neatly by rearranging layers inside (see the next drawing).

18. If you open the sides widely, you can wrap the layers around as shown here. Slowly and carefully collapse flat again.

19. Fold the upper triangular section downwards.

20. Fold the white flaps over the edge, crease firmly, and unfold. Open the layers slightly from the right.

21. Wrap the central flaps around so that they lie in the inside.

22. Fold the upper white edges inside to lie on the vertical edges.

23. Narrow the same flaps, again to the vertical edge.

24. Fold the next pair of flaps between the layers to the vertical.

25. Narrow them again.

26. Repeat step 22 on the next layers.

27. Repeat step 23 as well, for good luck.

28. Turn over and wrap a thin strip over and over.

29. Turn back over. Pleat the layers inside on existing creases. The hood folds towards you.

30. Here you make more delicate pleats. Flatten them firmly when complete.

31. Place a finger into the bottom pocket and carefully press down at the top. Encourage the model to spread out!

32. Complete.

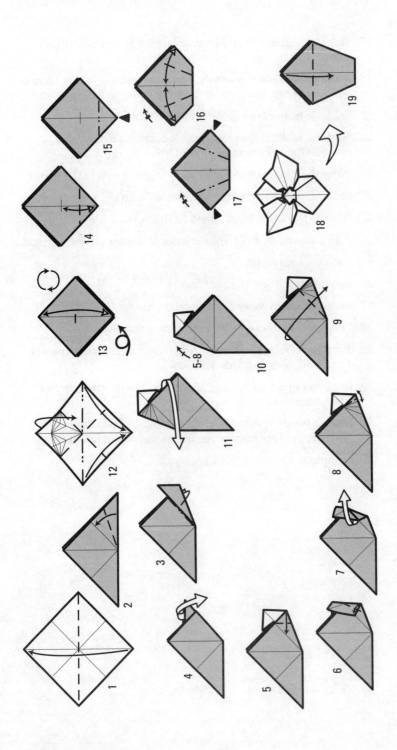

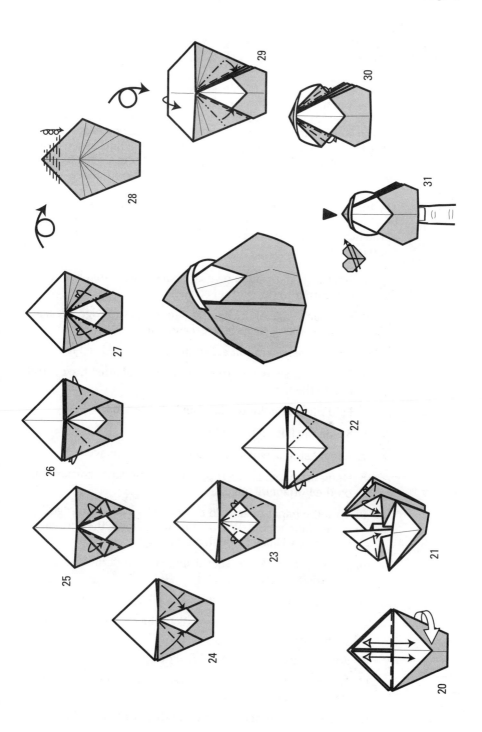

Aladdin

Max Hulme is well-known for his life-like animals and more geometric designs, but here he's come up with an unlikely flying model. I say 'unlikely' because it doesn't look as if it'll fly, but it does! Achieving a smooth gliding flight takes a little effort (although you might just strike lucky) but it's perfectly possible. Some techniques aren't the easiest of folds to do on a small flap, so practise the six steps from step 16 to 21 on a narrowed kite base using a separate sheet.

The British Origami Society has produced many booklets of members' work, including two devoted to Max's work, which you can buy at the BOS website www.britishorigami.info by clicking on the Supplies link.

1. Start with an upside down kite base, colour out. Fold the top corner to the bottom corner.

2. Fold each edge of the central flap to the top edge, creasing as far as the vertical centre. Unfold fully.

3. Start to make a rabbit ear in the centre, and keep it upright.

4. Fold the loose paper underneath as you flatten the central flap to the left.

5. Fold the first coloured layer in half upwards.

6. Swing the flap to the right.

7. Repeat step 5, which produces a colour change.

8. Open the paper at the top, swinging the inner corner to lie on the horizontal edge.

9. Turn the paper over. Fold the small flap over the edge, crease, and unfold. Where shown, reinforce the vertical crease as a valley through all the layers.

10. Turn the paper over. Tuck a small flap underneath using the existing crease.

11. Repeat steps 8 to 12 on the right side.

12. Fold the lower corner upwards to the centre. Rotate the paper 90 degrees.

13. Fold the upper half behind and down.

14. Focus on the white flap. Pre-crease and inside reverse the flap where shown.

15. Pull out the hidden layers on both sides to reveal the hand.

16. Reverse the top of the flap backwards.

17. Reverse it forwards again where shown.

18. Fold the head section over to the right.

19. Open and squash the head symmetrically.

20. Fold the raw edges out to the lower halves of the kite-shaped flap. At the same time, fold down and flatten the top corner.

21. Tuck the white corner inside with two small creases.

22. Turn the head to face forwards. Open and shape the body with curved, squashed creases. The body shrinks downwards slightly as you do this.

23. Make a slight curve in the centre of the model, hold it above you by the back of the rug, and gently release forwards. Fly to your heart's desire!

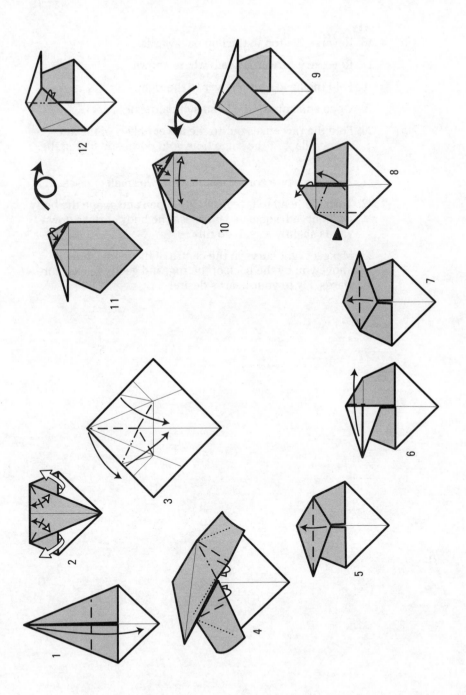

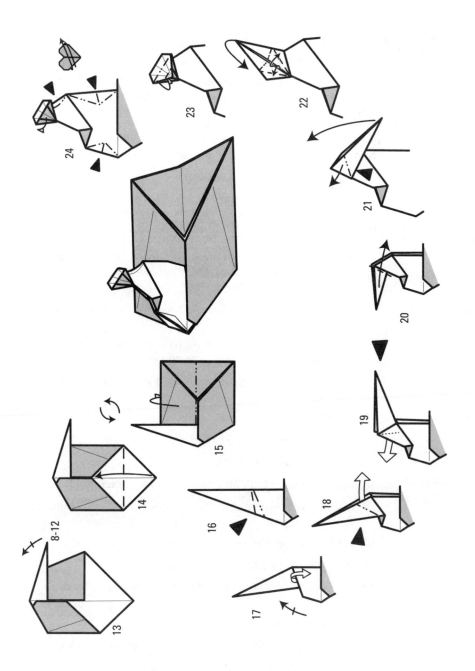

Beetle

Grzegorz Bubniak lives in a little hilly place called Lipinki situated in South Poland. His origami adventure started during his childhood when he folded simple models such as paper planes, traditional boats, or bangers. He bought his first origami book in his teens before discovering the enormous origami world on the Internet. You can check out his website for more information, at www.gregorigami.art.pl.

Start with a large square for your first few tries at this model; then see if you can manage a life-sized creepy-crawly! Fold as accurately as you can and be prepared to fold and refold in search of perfection.

1. Start with a waterbomb base, colour out (refer to Chapter 3 for the waterbomb base). Fold the lower right corner to the top.

2. Fold the outer edge to the vertical centre, crease, and unfold. Unfold the flap.

3. Form a rabbit's ear using the existing creases (some you need to swap from valley to mountain).

4. Fold the corner to the centre with a vertical crease. Crease and unfold.

5. Inside reverse the corner.

6. Fold the narrowed flap to the left.

7. Make another rabbit's ear.

8. Fold the flap in half, make a firm crease, and unfold.

9. Inside reverse the point. Max makes a closed sink here, but that's up to you!

10. Fold the lower flap out to the right.

11. Swing the flaps on the left over to the right.

12. One side is now complete. Repeat steps 3 to 11 on the other side.

13. This is the result. Turn the paper over.

14. Fold the upper edges at the top to the vertical centre.

15. Make a pleat through the body section.

16. This is an enlarged view. Make at least three pleats to form the body sections, and more if you're able!

17. Make a pleat at the lower end. Turn the paper over.

18. Fold the wings down and rotate the paper 180 degrees.

19. Open the wings by making the creases shown. The wings open and swing down to form a 3D wing case.

20. Curve the antennae as you like.

21. Complete and ready to scare small children.

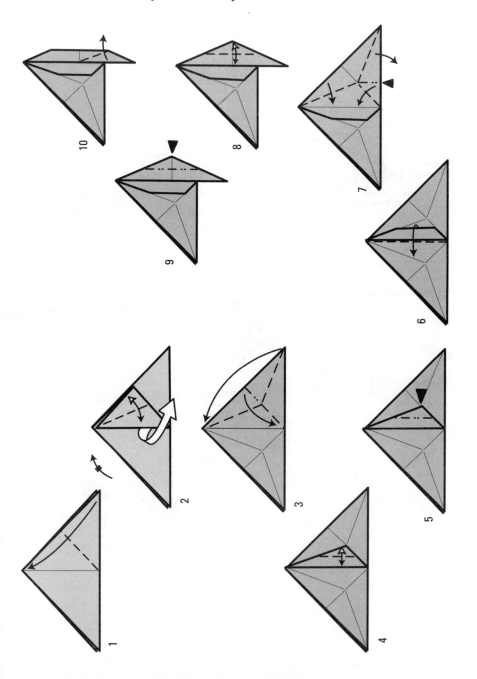

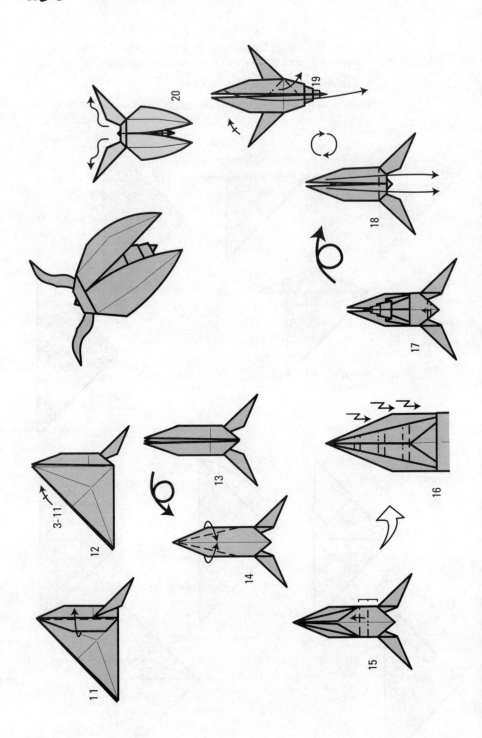

Mouse

Go Guspath lives in Hong Kong and he seems to have studied and absorbed most existing origami design techniques and used them to create extraordinary designs that show artistic flair and technical mastery.

This mouse is a challenging fold, but persevere! You need to focus on accurate creasing and be prepared to complete some of the steps in the air rather than on the table to achieve the 3D form. The result is a stylised but instantly recognisable mouse.

1. Start with a kite base, colour on the outside. Mark the quarter point (A) and then fold the outer corner to the quarter point, marking the outer ⅛ creases (B).

2. Fold the inner raw edge to lie on the ⅛ crease, crease, and unfold (A). Fold the same edge to the recent crease, crease, and unfold (B).

3. Fold the white triangular flap over the raw edges.

4. Starting the fold at the end of an existing crease, fold the corner over to lie somewhere on the raw edge. Crease and unfold, and repeat on the other side.

5. Fold the tip back to the left, starting the fold where the raw edge intersects a crease.

6. Unfold the upper half of the body.

7. Reverse the coloured flap inside, refolding the body inwards. In effect you're reversing the whole of the external corner.

8. Ease out the paper so that just the tip of the ear is revealed.

9. Make two mountain folds that start at the left centre and just touch the inside of the ears. Turn over and make a valley, checking the exact location. The folds should meet the edges of the body at the same distance!

10. Turn the paper over. Bisect the outer angles with a crease that just meets the creases you added in the last step.

11. Fold the sides of the tail to the horizontal centre, creasing just up to the existing creases. Turn the paper over.

12. Make a crease that starts at an internal crease intersection and meets the outer edge at right angles. Repeat on the matching side.

13. Put in the three long creases and pinch the sides together to form the short mountain creases. Check the next drawing to see what you're aiming for.

14. Hopefully this is what you've made so far!

15. Unfold back to a flat position. Ease out the paper from under the ear.

16. Make a small crimp on existing creases so that the paper can lie flat.

17. Partially open the paper on the creases shown – check step 19.

18. Here's an x-ray view of how the creases interact.

19. Remembering the paper is still 3D, fold the outer edge over – if you're lucky it should fit perfectly over the body, locking the 3D form into place.

20. This is what you're aiming for and, no, it's not easy! Once you've sussed it, repeat on the other flank.

21. Refold the tail as it was in step 14. Ease out the hidden paper from within the tail.

22. Fold the paper over to make the tail white. Repeat on the other side.

23. Fold the tip of the nose over.

24. Your mouse is ready to place on the table of an expensive restaurant.

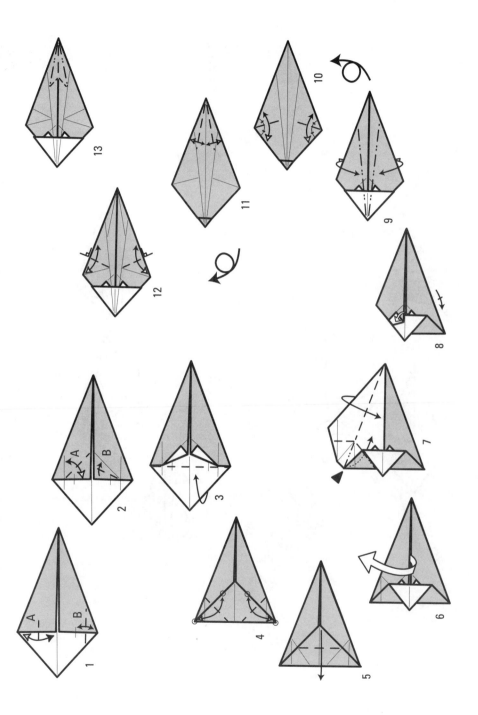

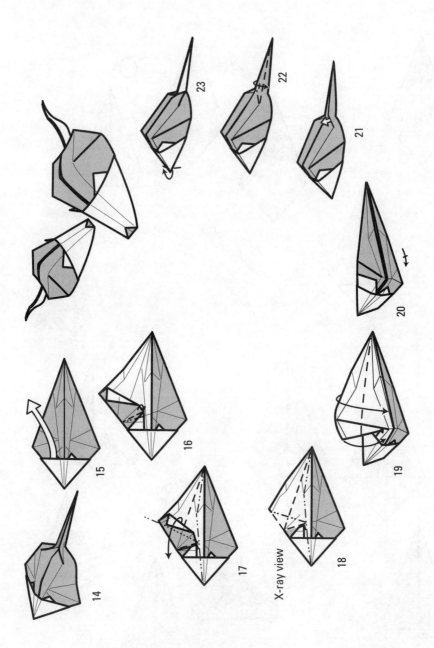

Part III
The Part of Tens

The 5th Wave   By Rich Tennant

"Oh, she makes all sorts of origami designs, but always seems intent on starting with a bird base."

In this part . . .

Every *For Dummies* book has a Part of Tens — a concise and quirky set of small but perfectly-formed chapters. Turn the page for lists of top tips, my favourite folders, and a whistle-stop tour of different styles of origami. Have fun!

Chapter 8

Ten Top Tips

*B*eing a former database programmer, I love lists – sorting them, querying them, and other such delights. The origami community spends inordinate amounts of time compiling lists and no one ever agrees on them.

Here are some top tips for your edification. I also throw in ten origami sayings for good measure. I'm just that kind of generous person.

Ten Folding Tips

Take this list to bed with you and recite it every night as a mantra to help you sleep:

✔ Accuracy is vital because errors multiply quickly.

✔ Always fold the paper away from you rather than towards you.

✔ Fold with clean hands.

✔ Folding an edge to an edge is easier than folding to a crease.

✔ If you get really stuck following a diagram, refold with a new sheet.

✔ Making a model is like rehearsing a piece of music – each takes practise to get right.

✔ Make sure your square is really square (measure it).

✔ Slow down and give yourself enough time to finish (a model always takes longer than you think).

- The first time you try a new design use a larger sheet than usual.
- To do a mountain fold, turn the paper over and do a valley.

Another Ten Tips

Here are more top tips to make your paper-folding life less stressful:

- A staple gun makes a handy alternative to glue. Yes, you are allowed to use glue sometimes!
- Always look ahead to the next drawing to see where you're going.
- Don't be afraid to experiment with a model.
- Have a waste-paper bin handy.
- Make rough diagrams of any models you make, otherwise you'll forget how to make them! Chapter 2 gives you lots of hints about diagramming.

Top ten origami sayings

For everyone who admires your skills, three cynics will think origami is a daft hobby and yearn to make a really clever pun at your expense. Prepare your snappy answers to this list and you'll put the cynics in their proper place.

- Are you a black belt?
- Do you get arrested for rustling?
- I invented that 20 years ago.
- Is your business in creasing or has the society folded?
- Isn't origami an Italian herb?
- My five-year-old would just love one of those!
- Sorry, it came apart in my hands *(at a display of modular origami)*
- You'll have us in creases soon.
- What is it?
- Would an origami display be a paper-view event?

✔ Save your origami mistakes because they may lead to new creative ideas.

✔ Sometimes you can make a fold as a soft crease, rather than a sharp one.

✔ Use a folded paper template to find angles and distances if you want to avoid unwanted creases. For examples of a template, see the Tulip Bowl in Chapter 5 and the Lazy Winston model in Chapter 4.

✔ If a model won't stay flat, leave it in the middle of a heavy book for a couple of days.

✔ Use a ruler and an old biro with no ink to score creases when you're folding twist boxes or similar, where you need greater accuracy.

Ten Things to Try If You Get Stuck

Everyone hits an origami brick wall sooner or later, but don't panic – here are a number of alternatives for you to try:

✔ Ask a friend to fold the model with you.

✔ Forget what you were folding, and make something else.

✔ Look at the next drawing and bodge it.

✔ Re-read the text more carefully.

✔ Throw away the model and start again.

✔ Try it again with a larger square.

✔ Have a cup of tea before coming back to it.

✔ Leave it overnight before coming back to it.

✔ Leave it a week before come back to it (and so on).

✔ Write to me and pay me to help you.

Chapter 9

Ten Styles of Origami

*L*ike any art form, origami has different approaches and philosophies. The more you fold, the more you'll find yourself drawn to one of these approaches.

Abstract

Abstract isn't just the category for any model you don't recognise. A few artistically-minded folders produce abstract folds that don't represent anything specific but are still intriguing and beautiful.

Crumpled

This technique was started by Paul Jackson (described in Chapter 10) and developed to extraordinary lengths by the Frenchman Vincent Floderer (www.le-crimp.org). The crumpled style involves a few simple origami techniques; mainly crumpling the paper into a ball many times before folding.

Modular

Modular origami is when you fold geometric units with flaps and pockets that tuck into each other. The end result should hold together without too much glue! Try your hand at the Modular Star model in Chapter 6.

Practical

Practical models are those that actually do something, such as envelopes, coasters, boxes, cups, dishes, and door-stoppers. Chapter 5 includes bowls and vases.

Pureland

Pureland origami is a concept developed by John Smith in the UK, who proposed a system using only mountain and valley creases (no reverses, sinks, and so on). The apparently restrictive limitations have produced a number of excellent designs.

Realistic

The emphasis in realistic origami is on creating an accurate model that has all the salient points of the original. For example, a six legged spider wouldn't be acceptable. Realistic origami generally results in complex designs with many, many steps.

Tessellations

With tessellations, you use varieties of twist techniques. You pre-crease the paper and fold it into tiles or tessellating patterns. The results are extraordinarily beautiful, but require a good technique both to crease and to fold.

Ultimate Realism

The style of ultimate realism wa founded in the 1970s by reclusive Norwegian Otto Nordstrom. Ultimate realism requires you to wrap paper tightly around the chosen subject (such as a moose), and then ease the contents out while preserving the shape in paper. Fun!

Virtual Origami

Virtual origami is the ultimate choice for lazy folders. Instead of making a model, you follow the diagrams in your head, perhaps twitching your fingers from time to time. You can then speak with authority about that design. Virtual origami is also a neat description for animated origami created using Flash software. For some great examples of animated origami, go the website www.origami. org.uk.

Wet Folding

Wet folding involves using paper made with glue (*sizing*) that holds the fibres of wood together. If you dampen the paper before folding, the glue dissolves slightly. As the paper dries, it sets, holding the paper in the form you've made. This enables you to fold the model in such a way that it keeps its roundness and 3D form.

Chapter 10

Ten Incredible Folders

In This Chapter

▶ Talented artists

▶ Software designers

▶ A Grand Master

*I*n this chapter are brief descriptions of my personal top ten folders whose work you can check out, if you want to know more. I've been lucky enough to meet all of these people and found them to be modest, approachable, and great ambassadors of origami. Most have been actively involved in their local origami society and travelled the world helping spread the origami gospel. Many have written origami books, so you can read and appreciate their contribution towards the art of origami.

David Brill

David is a British folder and artist. For over thirty years he has created some incredible work, showing a rare combination of technical and artistic mastery.

David has been folding and creating since the 1970s and is both former chairman and secretary (not at the same time!) of the British Origami Society. He is a well-known and much loved ambassador for origami all around the world. You can read his book *Brilliant Origami* (Japan Publications Trading Co.) and check out his website (www.brilliantorigami.com).

Tomoko Fuse

Tomoko is a Japanese folder who, for twenty years, has developed her own highly creative approach to origami, particularly modular designs such as boxes, stars, and polyhedra. She's written over sixty books, including *Fabulous Origami Boxes* and *Unit Origami:*

Multidimensional Transformations (both Japan Publications Trading Co.) which contain superb colourful and attractive designs.

Tomoko has travelled internationally, giving classes and creating extraordinary exhibitions. Her friendly and modest personality has made her a highly popular guest of all origami societies.

Paul Jackson

Paul is a British folder and artist, now living in Israel. Throughout his life he challenged origami precepts, producing beautiful and novel work. He places the beauty of origami far higher than any technical aspects and delights in simple action models.

He is married to Miri Golan, herself the Founder and Director of the Israeli Origami Center. Paul is a former editor of *British Origami* magazine and is the author of many books on the subject including Classic Origami (World Publications).

You can visit Paul's website at www.origami-artist.com. I also recommend you visit www.foldingtogether.org, the site of the Folding Together Project which brings together Israeli and Palestinian children to make origami models.

Eric Joisel

A French artist, Eric is perhaps best known for his human faces and figures, which show genuine and deep sensitivity and emotion. His long study of drawing and sculpting undoubtedly helps in his work. His 'folding touch' is almost impossible for mere mortals to replicate!

Eric has made numerous exhibitions around the world. His complex work is breathtaking: his legendary pangolin (scaly anteater) took months to create and over a week to fold – only two folded examples exist!

Check out Eric's book *3D Masks and Busts* (BOS Publications), and take a look at his website (which has a photo of the famous pangolin) at www.ericjoisel.com.

Robert Lang

Robert, an American, is a former laser-physicist who's recognised as a world leader in origami design and folding. He's been folding and creating for over 30 years. His work encompasses a wide variety of subjects including shells, flowers, insects, and animals.

Robert has revolutionised origami design with unique software to find folding locations (referencefinder) and to generate crease patterns for specific paper configurations (treemaker). Despite his many gifts, he remains modest and approachable. To find out more about his software and his designs, take a look at www.langorigami.com. To make his models, get hold of a copy of *Origami Design Secrets: Mathematical Methods for an Ancient Art* (A. K. Peters) or *Origami Insects* (Dover Publications).

Michael LaFosse

Michael, another American, breathes life into every fold he makes. Taking his inspiration from Master Akira Yoshizawa (described in this chapter), he creates flora and fauna of great beauty and artistry. He is a true paper artist, even making individual sheets of paper to fold a specific model with.

Take a look at www.origamido.com or read *Advanced Origami* (Tuttle Publishing) and *Origamido: The Art of Paper Folding* (Rockport Publishers Inc.).

Robert Neale

Since the late 1950s, Bob (an American) has created many innovative and influential designs in the 'simple' category. He brings his skills as a magician to some of his designs, offering tips on how to present a model with an exciting story. His work is never dull!

Hundreds of creators produce complex technical designs, but precious few focus on the opposite end of the folding spectrum. Creating a top quality simple design is surprisingly difficult, but Bob has managed it for many years. His books include *Which Came First* (BOS Publications) and *Origami Plain and Simple* (St Martin's Press).

Philip Shen

Philip was born in the Philippines, moved to Hong Kong, and then America. He died in 2004. For over 40 years he produced geometric designs showing great depth and beauty. He liked to work with simple crease patterns to see how the creases could be folded most naturally and not forced into place. This method resulted in designs that usually had a 3D form and took advantage of the tension within paper.

Philip's work isn't widely known, but is hugely respected by those in the know. You can see his models in *Selected Geometric Folds* and *More Geometric Folds* (BOS Publications).

Herman Van Goubergen

Herman is a Belgian creator. He insists that each new model he designs incorporates some innovative and original aspect. He sets himself such high standards that he often only unveils one design per year, but it's always worth the wait.

You can find details of his work on the Origami database site at http//db.origami.com.

Akira Yoshizawa

Akira Yoshizawa is the Japanese Grand Master of origami, and largely responsible for origami as we know it. He claims to have created over 50,000 designs, of which only a relatively small fraction have been published. His life-long study of the art, artistic touch, and humility set high standards for all other folders.

Yoshizawa acted as a world-wide cultural ambassador for Japan throughout his life. In 1983, the Japanese emperor Hirohito awarded him the Order of the Rising Sun, one of the highest awards that can be given to a Japanese citizen. He died in 2005.

Yoshizawa's books include *Origami Museum (Animals v. 1)* (Japan Publications Trading Co.) and you can find out more about him at www008.upp.so-net.ne.jp/origami-ios.

Index

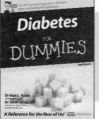

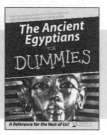

FOR DUMMIES®

The easy way to get more done and have more fun

LANGUAGES

978-0-7645-5194-9

978-0-7645-5193-2

978-0-7645-5196-3

MUSIC

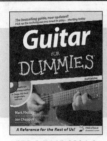

978-0-7645-9904-0

978-0-470-03275-6
UK Edition

978-0-7645-5105-5

SCIENCE & MATHS

978-0-7645-5326-4

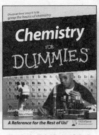

978-0-7645-5430-8

978-0-7645-5325-7

Art For Dummies
978-0-7645-5104-8

Baby & Toddler Sleep Solutions For
Dummies
978-0-470-11794-1

Bass Guitar For Dummies
978-0-7645-2487-5

Christianity For Dummies
978-0-7645-4482-8

Filmmaking For Dummies
978-0-7645-2476-9

Forensics For Dummies
978-0-7645-5580-0

German For Dummies
978-0-7645-5195-6

Hobby Farming For Dummies
978-0-470-28172-7

Jewelry Making & Beading For
Dummies
978-0-7645-2571-1

Judaism For Dummies
978-0-7645-5299-1

Knitting for Dummies, 2nd Edition
978-0-470-28747-7

Music Composition For Dummies
978-0-470-22421-2

Physics For Dummies
978-0-7645-5433-9

Sex For Dummies, 3rd Edition
978-0-470-04523-7

Solar Power Your Home For Dummies
978-0-470-17569-9

Tennis For Dummies
978-0-7645-5087-4

The Koran For Dummies
978-0-7645-5581-7

U.S. History For Dummies
978-0-7645-5249-6

Wine For Dummies, 4th Edition
978-0-470-04579-4

**Available wherever books are sold. For more information or to order direct go to
www.wiley.com or call +44 (0) 1243 843291**